D1141102

# ᴛʜᴇReflexology
## MANUAL

**Pauline Wills** BRA, BSY, H.Dip.C.Th., IACT* qualified as a reflexologist in 1980 through the Bayly School of Reflexology, London. Prior to this she studied the discipline of yoga through several different schools before qualifying as a teacher. She is also a colour practitioner, studying with both the Maitreya School of Mental Colour Healing and The Hygeia College of Colour Therapy. Four years ago she was given the idea of combining colour with reflexology. From her research into this her book, *The Reflexology and Colour Therapy Workbook*, was born. She is now involved in teaching reflexologists how to use colour in conjunction with reflexology in both the UK and Ireland. She runs a successful reflexology and colour therapy practice, teaches yoga and colour therapy and gives talks and workshops throughout Europe. She has also written books on colour therapy and visualization, and a book with Theo Gimbel on yoga and colour.

*Abbreviations*
*BRA: British Reflexology Association*
*BSY: British School of Yoga*
*H.Dip.C.Th.: Hygeia Diploma of Colour Therapy*
*IACT: International Association of Colour Therapy*

# THE Reflexology MANUAL

*A photographic
step-by-step guide to treating the body
through the feet and hands*

## PAULINE WILLS

Photography by
Sue Atkinson

HEADLINE

*This book is dedicated to Reginald Money for all the help and support that he gave me whilst writing it.*

PLEASE NOTE

This book is not intended as guidance for the treatment of serious health problems; please refer to a medical professional if you are in any doubt about any aspect of a person's condition.

Text copyright © Pauline Wills 1995
Photographs copyright © Sue Atkinson 1995
This edition copyright © Eddison Sadd Editions 1995

The right of Pauline Wills to be identified as the author of this work has been asserted by her in accordance with the British Copyright, Design and Patents Act 1988.

This edition published in 1995 by BCA by arrangement with HEADLINE BOOK PUBLISHING

CN 1693

All rights reserved. No part of this publication may be reproduced, stored in a retrieval system, or transmitted, in any form or by any means without the prior written permission of the publisher, nor be otherwise circulated in any form of binding or cover other than that in which it is published and without a similar condition being imposed upon the subsequent purchaser.

5 7 9 8 6 4

AN EDDISON·SADD EDITION
Edited, designed and produced by
Eddison Sadd Editions Limited

Phototypeset in Garamond ITC Light and Garamond ITC Light Condensed
using QuarkXPress on Apple Macintosh
Origination by Rainbow Graphic Arts, Hong Kong
Printed and bound in China by Shenzhen Donnelley Bright Sun

# Contents

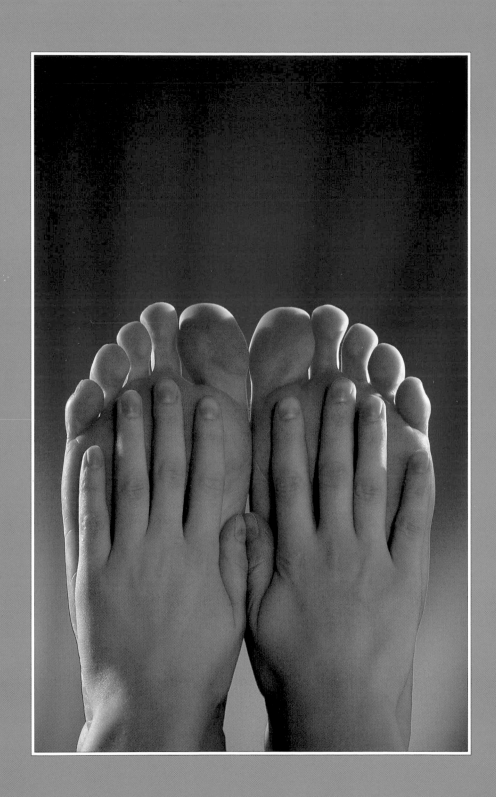

# 1

# What is reflexology?

Originally known as reflex zone therapy, reflexology is a holistic healing method which involves pressure and massage of the reflex points found on the feet and hands. The dictionary defines the word *reflex* as 'an involuntary muscle contraction due to an external stimulus'. In the context of reflexology, however, reflex is used in the sense of *reflection*, or mirror image. These reflexes are found on the soles of the feet, or the palms of the hands, which act as small 'mirrors' *reflecting* the whole organism.

Reflexology teaches that a vital energy, or life force, circulates between the organs of the body, permeating every living cell and tissue. If this energy becomes blocked, the part of the body relating to the blockage is affected. Energy blocks in the human body are reflected on the hands and feet in one or more of the zones located there. By using specific pressure techniques, they can be detected through the experience of pain, or through the presence of 'gritty areas', often referred to as crystal deposits. These occur in the part of the foot or hand that relates to the part of the body that is imbalanced. The pressure and massage techniques taught in reflexology are designed to dissipate energy blocks, and break down crystalline structure. Through stimulation of the circulatory and lymphatic systems, and by encouraging the release of toxins, reflexology promotes the body to heal itself.

Apart from treating disease, reflexology is an extremely effective therapy in cases of stress, tension and tiredness. And, like acupuncture, it can also be used as a preventive measure against ill health.

*Opposite Reflexology is about giving and receiving. Here, energy is transmitted to the patient through the hands of the therapist and information is received from the patient's feet.*

# The history of reflexology

The origin of reflexology, or zone therapy as it was called, still remains a mystery. In his book, *Zone Therapy*, Dr William Fitzgerald states that 'a form of treatment by means of pressure points was known in India and China 5,000 years ago. This knowledge, however, appears to be lost or forgotten. Perhaps it was set aside in favour of acupuncture, which emerged as the stronger growth from the same root.' Another conjecture is that it began in Egypt. Evidence for this stems from an Egyptian tomb drawing dating back to 2330 BC This drawing depicts four people; one person is being treated with foot massage and a second person with hand massage. Others credit its birth to the Incas, a people who belonged to a very ancient Peruvian civilization, possibly reaching back to 12,000 BC. It is speculated that they passed down their knowledge of zone therapy to the North American Indians who are still using this form of treatment today.

What is certain is that zone therapy was being used as far back as AD 1500. Cellini (1500–1571), the great Florentine sculptor, is reported to have used strong pressure on his fingers and toes in order to relieve pain in his body with apparent success. The American president, James Abram Garfield (1831–81), who was the victim of an assassination attempt, is said to have alleviated the resulting pain by applying pressure to certain points on his feet. During the sixteenth century, several books on zone therapy were published in Europe. One of these was written by Dr Adamus and Dr A'tatis. Shortly after it appeared on the market, a similar book was published by Dr Ball in Leipzig.

The credit for initiating reflexology as it is known today must be given to Dr William Fitzgerald. Born in 1872, he graduated in medicine at the University of Vermont, USA, in 1895. After practising in hospitals in Vienna, Paris and London, he became an ear, nose and throat specialist and settled in Connecticut. While working in Vienna, he studied the work of Dr H. Bresslar, who had researched the link between pressure points on the feet and the internal organs of the body and published his findings in a book, *Zone Therapy*. Interestingly, Dr Bresslar mentions that therapeutic foot massage was practised during the fourteenth century.

Above *Hand massage. Detail from a relief on Ankhamor's tomb at Saqqara, Egypt.*

# The longitudinal zones

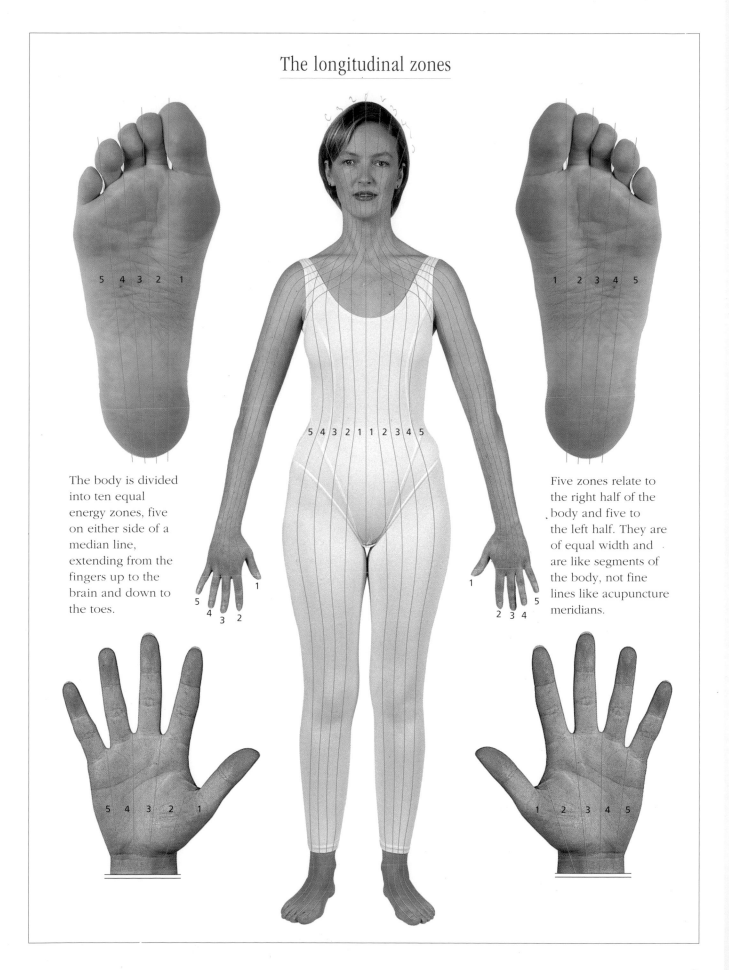

The body is divided into ten equal energy zones, five on either side of a median line, extending from the fingers up to the brain and down to the toes.

Five zones relate to the right half of the body and five to the left half. They are of equal width and are like segments of the body, not fine lines like acupuncture meridians.

Dr Fitzgerald started to practise zone therapy techniques on his patients. To apply pressure, he used rubber bands, clamps and probes. He discovered that pressure applied to some parts of the foot induced anaesthesia in specific parts of the body. His continuing research led him to formulate the division of the body into ten equal longitudinal energy zones – five relating to the right half of the body and five to the left half – by drawing an imaginary line from the top of the head down through the centre of the body.

These ten energy zones terminate on the soles of the feet and the palms of the hands. Zone one incorporates the thumb, extends up the arm into the shoulders and neck to the brain, and then down the body to the big toe. Zone two extends from the index finger, up the arm into the shoulders, neck and brain and down the body to the second toe. The third zone extends from the middle finger, up the arm to the shoulder, neck and brain, then down the body to the third toe. The fourth zone begins with the ring finger, travelling up the arm into the shoulder, neck and brain, then down the body to the fourth toe. The fifth zone extends from the little finger, travelling up the arm to the shoulder, neck and brain and down the body to the fifth toe.

In 1916 Dr Edwin Bowers, Dr Fitzgerald's colleague, publicly described the treatment propounded by Dr Fitzgerald, referring to it as 'zone therapy'. A year later their combined work appeared in a book entitled *Zone Therapy*. It contained treatment suggestions and recommendations for doctors, dentists, gynaecologists, ear, nose and throat specialists and chiropractors. The first edition included diagrams of the reflexes of the feet and the corresponding ten zones of the body. Dr Fitzgerald soon began to give courses on this method of treatment to medical practitioners.

These theories were not enthusiastically received by the medical profession in general, but one doctor, Joseph Shelby Riley, was so impressed that both he and his wife – also a doctor – attended Fitzgerald's courses on zone therapy in order to use it in their own practice. It was an assistant of Joseph Riley, Eunice Ingham (1879–1974), who instigated what we know today as reflexology.

Through her dedicated research, Eunice Ingham was able to correlate the anatomical structure of the body with the energy zones located on the feet, and found that the feet provided a mirror image of the entire body. She also found that the greater sensitivity of the feet enhanced treatment. Because of this, reflexology treatment is generally carried out on the feet rather than on the hands.

Eunice Ingham travelled extensively for many years, teaching and sharing her knowledge with complementary therapists such as masseurs, osteopaths and naturopaths. During her lifetime she wrote two books: *Stories the Feet Can Tell* and *Stories the Feet Have Told*. In 1960 one of her students, Doreen Bayly, introduced reflexology to Great Britain, where she started a training school of reflexology. She also ran courses in Europe.

From its early beginnings, reflexology has developed a more scientific background based on ever increasing knowledge of anatomy and physiology. This has helped its acceptance into conventional, orthodox medicine: many countries have recognized reflexology associations. Today, reflexology is a fast-growing therapy worldwide.

# How does reflexology work?

Reflexology, sometimes still referred to as zone therapy, is based on Dr Fitzgerald's concept of the zone system. Ten separate energy currents circulate – five in each half of the body – between the head and the toes and the five fingers. These currents flow in longitudinal lines called zones. Within these zones lie all the organs and muscles of the body, as shown in the diagram overleaf.

In 1970 a German reflexologist, Hanne Marquarett, author of *Reflex Zone Therapy of the Feet*, felt that it would be easier to locate the reflexes found on the feet if the human form was further divided into three transverse zones. She did this by drawing three imaginary lines across the physical body, which corresponded to three imaginary lines placed across the feet. In this way, the feet provided a miniature map consisting of ten longitudinal and three transverse zones. This made for greater precision in locating the different reflexes. On the hands, because of the way they are constructed, only the second transverse line can be drawn *(see page 13)*.

The first transverse zone in the body is found at the level of the shoulder girdle and relates to the head and neck. On the feet, all reflexes relating to this part of the body are found above the first transverse line – the shoulder girdle. The second transverse zone lies at waist level and relates to the structure of the chest and upper abdomen. All reflexes pertaining to this part of the body are found between the first and second transverse line – the waist line – on the feet. On the hands, reflexes pertaining to the chest, upper abdomen, neck and head are found above the second transverse line.

The third transverse zone in the body runs across the pelvic girdle and relates to the lower abdomen and pelvis. All reflexes associated with this part of the body are found between the second and third transverse line – pelvic girdle – on the feet; and below the second transverse line on the hands.

When the energy currents that flow through the longitudinal zones build up at certain points, they create an accumulation of energy, or blockage, at those points. Referred to as energy blocks, they interrupt the smooth flow of energy throughout the body, causing the pain, disorder, disease or whatever problems which require healing.

Above *To treat the spinal reflex, the pressure-point technique used is known as sliding.*

# Position of the organs of the body within the zones

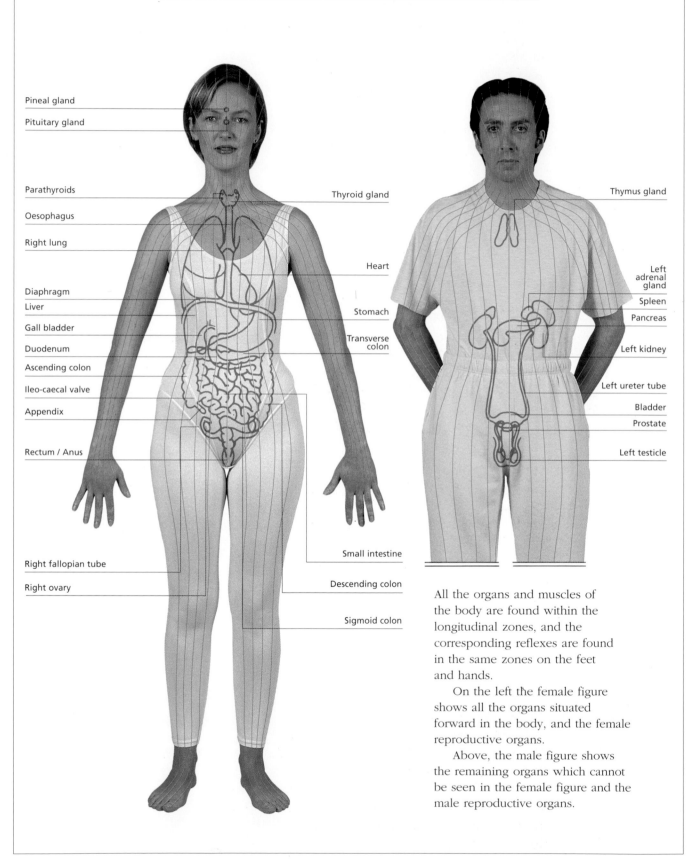

Pineal gland

Pituitary gland

Parathyroids

Oesophagus

Right lung

Diaphragm

Liver

Gall bladder

Duodenum

Ascending colon

Ileo-caecal valve

Appendix

Rectum / Anus

Right fallopian tube

Right ovary

Thyroid gland

Heart

Stomach

Transverse colon

Small intestine

Descending colon

Sigmoid colon

Thymus gland

Left adrenal gland

Spleen

Pancreas

Left kidney

Left ureter tube

Bladder

Prostate

Left testicle

All the organs and muscles of the body are found within the longitudinal zones, and the corresponding reflexes are found in the same zones on the feet and hands.

On the left the female figure shows all the organs situated forward in the body, and the female reproductive organs.

Above, the male figure shows the remaining organs which cannot be seen in the female figure and the male reproductive organs.

Reflexology, by using specific massage and pressure techniques on the reflexes of the feet or hands, is able to remove the energy blocks. The energy currents flow freely once more, and the body is returned to harmony.

However, energy blocks in the zones can have many causes: stress, bad diet, a life style that is no longer beneficial, a broken marriage or relationship to name but a few. The way to successfully dissipate the problem is to find the cause. Reflexology is a holistic therapy, and techniques must be coupled with counselling by the reflexologist – and in some cases by a qualified counsellor.

Of course, this may take many hours of counselling. A cause may well be buried deep in the subconscious mind because a person finds it too painful to cope with. Or some people, although they are well aware of the cause, may nonetheless be unwilling to discuss it simply because they are not psychologically prepared to resolve it.

Yet these energy blocks are obstacles which must be overcome. If the cause is not found, a patient will continue to block the energy which the reflexologist has started to release. Equally, if the cause is known but the patient is unwilling to deal with it, the energy channels which the reflexologist frees will be blocked again by the patient.

In conventional medicine, a patient is given a prescription and is not expected to take any responsibility for him or herself. Complementary medicine – which reflexology is – takes a holistic approach: the patient is involved, and is expected to take responsibility together with the therapist to effect a cure. Of course, as the term implies, complementary therapies can work very well as a complement to allopathic medicine.

Reflexology treatment centres on massage and pressure to the reflex areas in the feet and hands. Therefore it is important to learn the anatomy of those parts of the physical body. And since the position of the transverse zones on the feet and hands has a direct relationship with their skeletal structure, it is essential to study this structure in some detail so as to be able to locate the reflex areas accurately.

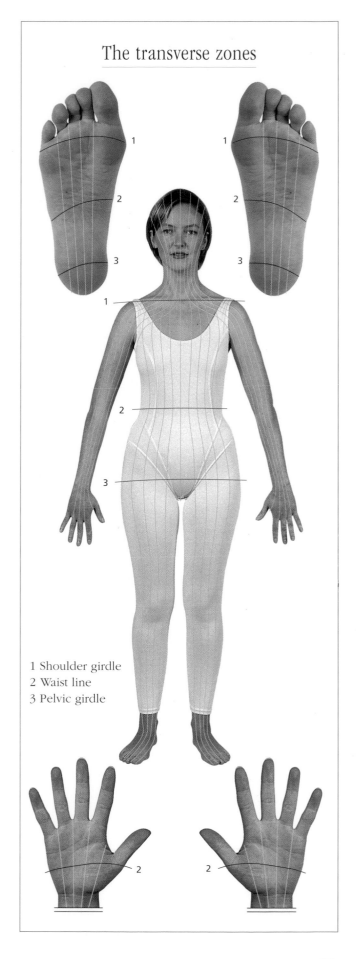

## The transverse zones

1 Shoulder girdle
2 Waist line
3 Pelvic girdle

# The structure of the feet

Each foot is made up of twenty-six bones and thirty-three articulations. They are joined together by over a hundred ligaments. The twenty-six bones are (from heel to toes): the calcaneum; the talus; the navicular; the cuboid; three cuneiform bones; five metatarsals and fourteen phalanges (two in the big toe and three in each of the remaining four toes).

The posterior part of the foot contains the talus and the calcaneum; the anterior part of the foot comprises the cuboid, navicular and three cuneiform bones. The word *cuneiform* means wedge-shaped; these three bones are referred to as the medial, intermediate and lateral cuneiform. All these bones are called the tarsal bones.

The talus is the only bone in the foot that articulates with the fibula and tibia bones of the leg. In the act of walking, the talus bears the entire weight of the body. Part of this weight is then transmitted to the calcaneum – or heelbone – and the remainder of the tarsal bones. The calcaneum is the largest and strongest bone in the foot.

The five metatarsal bones are long bones and each consists of a base, a shaft and a head. The base of the first three articulates with the first, second and third cuneiform bones, and that of the lateral two with the cuboid. The first metatarsal bone, being thicker than the rest, bears more weight.

Like the metatarsal bones, the phalanges consist of a proximal base, a middle shaft and a distal head. The big toe consists of two large, heavy phalanges known as the proximal and distal phalanges. The other four toes each consists of three phalanges.

The bones of the feet form two arches: the longitudinal and the transverse arch. The longitudinal arch consists of a medial part (facing inwards) and a lateral part (facing outwards). The arches enable the foot to support the weight of the body and provide leverage while walking. The bones which make them up are held by tendons and ligaments.

The muscles of the foot are intricate and comparable to those of the hand; but whereas the muscles in the hand are designed for precise and intricate movement, those of the foot are limited to support and locomotion.

In relationship to the skeletal structure of the feet, the first transverse zone covers the phalanges, which lie above the shoulder girdle line. The second transverse zone covers the metatarsals and lies between the shoulder

# Bone structure of the feet

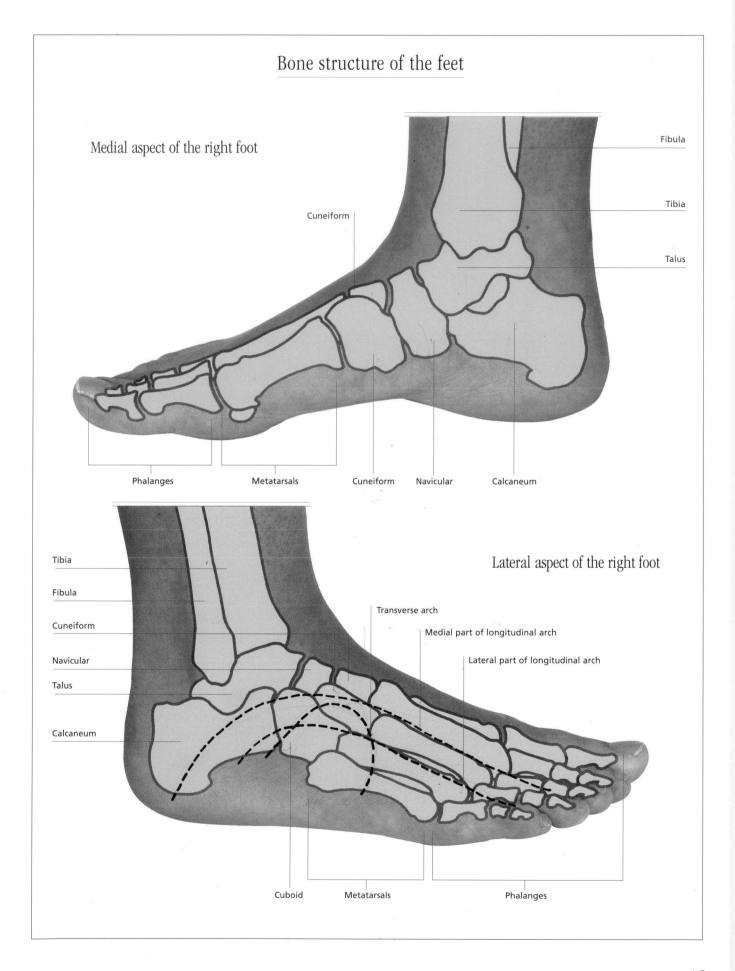

Medial aspect of the right foot

Cuneiform

Fibula

Tibia

Talus

Phalanges

Metatarsals

Cuneiform

Navicular

Calcaneum

Tibia

Fibula

Cuneiform

Navicular

Talus

Calcaneum

Lateral aspect of the right foot

Transverse arch

Medial part of longitudinal arch

Lateral part of longitudinal arch

Cuboid

Metatarsals

Phalanges

# Bone structure of the feet

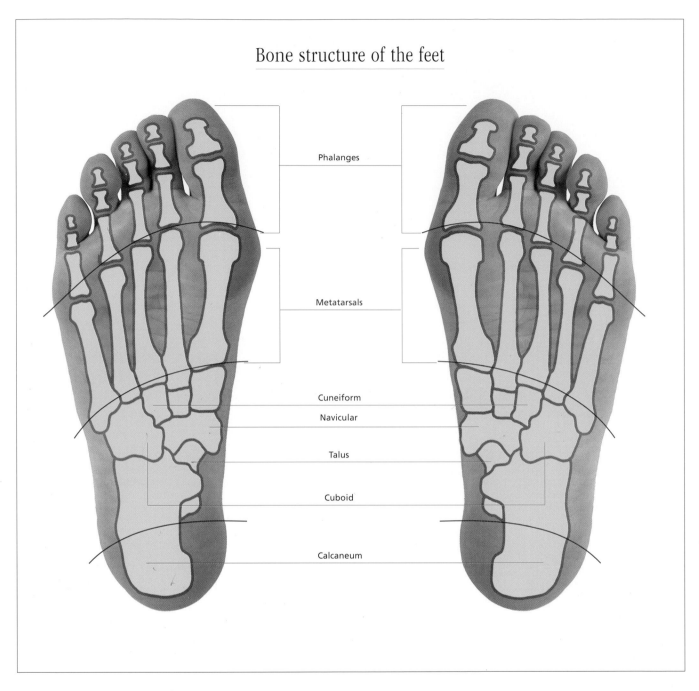

Phalanges

Metatarsals

Cuneiform

Navicular

Talus

Cuboid

Calcaneum

girdle line and the waist line. The third transverse zone, the pelvic floor, is found below the waist line lying midway between the calcaneum and talus bones.

## Problems relating to the feet

Many disorders relating to the feet are encountered in the course of practising reflexology. Since they may affect the treatment in different ways, it is very important to have some knowledge of them and to know how to distinguish them.

**Athlete's foot** A harmless condition, caused by a fungus growing in the skin between and under the toes – especially between the fourth and fifth toes. The skin becomes red, flaky and itchy. The fungus can also affect other parts of the foot, and the toenails. If the nails are infected, they become thicker and yellow.

**Bunions** An inflamed bag of fluid overlying a bony protrusion from the outside edge of the joint, at the base of the big toe. The medical name for a bunion is *hallux valgus*. Bunions tend to occur in people with an inherited weakness in toe joints, or who wear ill-fitting shoes. Shoes with high heels and pointed toes are great promoters of this condition. The result of the inflammation is that the bony base of the big toe is twisted and the toe is pushed out beyond the normal outline of the foot, forming what is known as a bunion.

**Chilblains** An acute or chronic form of injury caused by exposure to cold. People who suffer these normally have an exaggerated sensitivity to cold. A chilblain is characterized by inflammation of the skin, itching and swelling, frequently followed by blisters.

**Claw foot** A condition in which the medial longitudinal arch is abnormally elevated. It is frequently caused by muscle imbalance, which could arise from poliomyelitis.

**Club foot** A foot that is twisted out of shape so that the sole does not rest on the floor when standing. It is a condition that some babies are born with and is thought to be caused by the fetus maintaining a fixed position in the uterus for a long period.

**Corns and calluses** Areas of skin that have thickened as a result of constant pressure. Corns are small and develop on the toes; calluses are larger and usually develop on the soles of the feet.

**Flat feet** At birth, a normal baby has flat feet. The arches of the feet develop slowly over the first six years of its life. When this condition develops in adults, it is usually due to the weakening of the muscles or tendons that support the bones which make up the arches of the feet. If these tendons and muscles are weakened, the medial longitudinal arch may decrease in height until the foot is flat.

**March fracture** This can occur in one or more of the metatarsal bones after prolonged or repeated periods of excessive stress on the feet. It most commonly occurs in walkers and runners, and produces pain in the ball of the foot that worsens on exertion.

**Tarsal tunnel syndrome** This condition occurs when nerves become entrapped at the ankle. The principal symptom is an intermittent burning pain or numbness in the sole or toes of the affected foot which may spread to the calf. The problem can be made worse by standing or walking.

**Verrucas** *Verruca* is the Latin word for wart. On the sole of the foot, it is called *verruca plantaris*. In appearance, verrucas are small, hard, whitish or flesh-coloured lumps with a cauliflower-like surface. They contain small clotted blood vessels that resemble black splinters. Through walking they tend to be pushed into the foot and become painful. Several verrucas can appear close to each other, scanning a width of 2.5 centimetres (1 in) or more.

## Foot care

To have problem-free feet, it is essential to take good care of them. First, it is important to wear well-fitting shoes.Whenever possible, walk barefoot. It stimulates the reflexes on the feet, thereby stimulating the energy flow in the whole body. If prone to developing corns or calluses, regular visits to the chiropodist are advisable, in order to have the formation of hard skin removed. Hard skin can affect the reflex that it covers. Through wearing tight shoes or cutting the toenails in a curve rather than straight across, ingrowing toenails can occur. If not dealt with, these can press into the head reflex on the toe and cause headaches. Nails should be trimmed regularly with scissors or special nail clippers; a good time is after a bath when they are fairly soft. Bathe the feet at least twice a day and apply a good foot cream to prevent the skin becoming dry.

# The structure of the hands and wrists

Each hand and wrist comprises twenty-seven bones and tendons. The latter attach the muscles to bone. The twenty-seven bones consist of: eight carpals; five metacarpals and fourteen phalanges.

The eight carpals constitute the wrist, or carpus. They are small bones and are arranged in two rows of four. The row nearest the radius and ulna bones of the arm includes the scaphoid (resembles a boat), lunate (resembles a crescent moon), triquetrum (has three articular surfaces) and pisiform (pea-shaped). The row nearest the metacarpals comprises the trapezium (four-sided), trapezoid (also four-sided), capitate (the rounded head of which articulates with the lunate) and hamate (named for the large hook-shaped projection on its anterior surface).

The five metacarpal bones form the palm of the hand. The heads of these bones are commonly called the knuckles and are very easily visible when the fist is clenched. The phalanges are the bones found in the four fingers and thumb. The index finger, middle finger, ring finger and little finger consists of three phalanges each, but the thumb – like the big toe – has only two.

The muscles that move the wrist, hand and fingers are many and varied. They include anterior muscles which function as flexors; posterior muscles which act as extensors; and intrinsic muscles. The intrinsic muscles are located in the palm of the hand and they help in the movement of the fingers.

The efficiency of the hands depends before all on the movement of the thumb, its functional importance only being realized when it is put out of action through injury. The general functions of the hand are: power grip (forcible movement of the fingers and thumbs against the palm of the hand, like squeezing); precision handling (a change in the position of an object that requires exactly controlled finger and thumb motions, as in winding a watch or threading a needle), and pinch (compression between the index finger and the thumb or between the thumb and first two fingers). When carrying out a reflexology treatment, all of these movements are utilized.

## Problems relating to the hands

**Carpal tunnel syndrome** The carpal tunnel is formed by the wrist bones and a tough membrane on the underside of the wrist which binds the bones together. Through this tunnel runs the nerve which carries signals between the hand and the brain. If, for a number of

## Bone structure of the hands

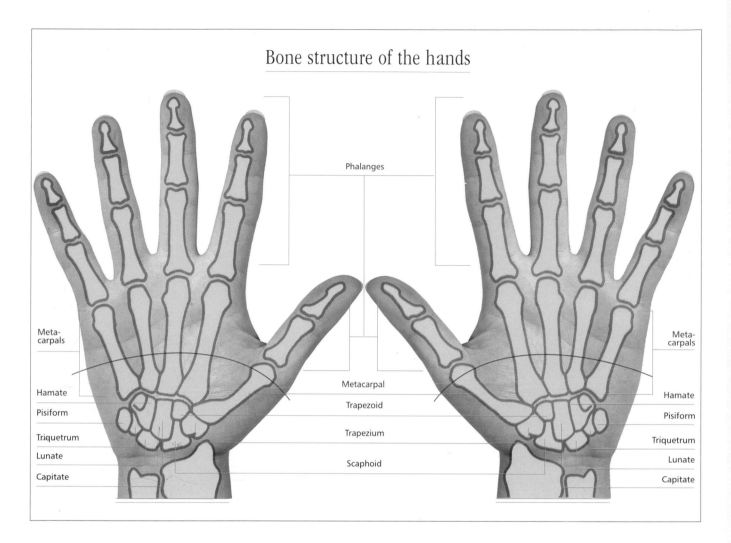

Phalanges

Meta-
carpals

Hamate

Pisiform

Triquetrum

Lunate

Capitate

Metacarpal

Trapezoid

Trapezium

Scaphoid

Meta-
carpals

Hamate

Pisiform

Triquetrum

Lunate

Capitate

reasons, the tissues within the carpal tunnel swell, they press on and pinch the nerve. The symptoms are tingling and intermittent numbness of the hand, frequently accompanied by pains radiating up the arm from the wrist.

**Chilblains** (*see* Problems relating to the feet *page 16*).

**Clubbed fingers** A syndrome of chronic lung disease. The reason why this disease causes this deformity of the fingers is not known. The symptoms are disappearing cuticles and curving fingernails around the end of the fingers. The tips of the fingers may also flatten out to become spatula shaped.

**Dupuytren's contracture** This occurs when the layer of tough fibrous tissue that lies under the skin on the palm of the hand, thickens and shrinks. The shrinkage eventually

causes the ring finger and little finger to be permanently bent at the knuckles. Some sufferers also have thickened skin pads over their other knuckles and on the balls of their feet. This is a common condition in men over forty, and tends to be hereditary.

**Fingernails** Deformation or discolouration can be caused by injury or illness. In some cases of psoriasis of the hands (a chronic disease of the skin of unknown origin), the nails tend to become thick, pitted and separated from the underneath skin. Paronychia is an infection of the skin adjacent to a nail caused by either bacteria or yeast microbes – a type of fungus – and occurs particularly in people who spend a lot of time with their hands in water. It causes the nail fold to become swollen, red and painful. The cuticle may lift away from the base of the nail, expelling pus on pressure. Occasionally, however, the nails themselves are attacked by this fungus and become thick, rigid and discoloured.

Iron deficiency anaemia can make nails spoon-shaped; lung cancer and congenital heart disorders can cause clubbing. Discoloration of the nails can be caused by various disorders. The nail bed appears pale in the case of anaemia, and white in some forms of liver disease. Small, black, splinter-like areas appear under the nails in infections of the heart valves. An accidental knock to the nail can cause one or more small white patches to appear.

**Ganglion** A swelling which appears under the skin, either in the wrist or on the upper part of the foot. Its development is due to the accumulation of a small amount of a jelly-like substance in a joint capsule or a tendon, causing it to swell. The size of ganglia varies. Usually they are no larger than a pea, and can be either soft or quite hard. They are usually painless, or the cause of only slight discomfort. Unless obtrusive or uncomfortable, they are best left alone and frequently disappear by themselves.

**Osteoarthritis** The cause of osteoarthritis is unknown. It occurs in the joints of the body, including the finger joints. The smooth lining of the bones – where they come into contact – begins to flake or crack. As the cartilage deteriorates, the underlying bone is affected and may become thickened and distorted, making movement painful and restricted. The symptoms of this disorder are swelling and stiffness in the affected joint which can occur over a period of months or years.

**Raynaud's disease** A circulatory disorder affecting fingers and occasionally toes. For some reason which is still unknown, the small arteries which provide the indispensable blood supply to the fingers become hypersensitive to cold. As a result, they suddenly contract, thereby reducing the flow of blood to the affected area. The lack of oxygenated blood to the affected area gives it a pale and sometimes bluish appearance.

**Tenosynovitis** Its popular name is triggerfinger. It is caused by the synovium, the membrane that sheaths the tendons of the fingers and thumbs and assists freedom of movement, becoming inflamed and swollen. In time this will heal, but it may become tight or narrow as it does so, resulting in restricted movement of the tendons and making it difficult to straighten the affected fingers. The area over the tendon becomes painful and tender. In addition, the affected finger or thumb will hurt and may make a crackling sound whenever it is moved.

## Hand care

Before starting a reflexology treatment, it is worthwhile examining the hands and nails of the person receiving treatment. These will frequently give some indication as to the general state of health.

It is also important for reflexologists to care for their own hands and fingers. Remember that these are the tools of the trade. Always make sure that your hands are thoroughly dried after washing, and wear protective gloves when washing up and cleaning. Lastly, always apply a good quality hand cream after washing your hands and before going to bed. This will keep them soft and supple. If you follow these few simple rules, your hands should remain healthy and strong.

Finally, when working with reflexology, it is esential to acquire the correct pressure and massage techniques. People who constantly use their fingers and thumbs, especially if used in a way that puts strain on the joints and ligaments, could become prone to tenosynovitis, (triggerfinger) or osteoarthritis. Also, make sure that your nails are kept short and clean. Patients will not thank you if you constantly dig your nails into them during treatment. Likewise, they could be offended if they see you with dirty nails.

# Pressure-point techniques

Before attempting a full reflexology treatment, it is vital that you have mastered all the techniques you will be using, in order to feel confident that you are performing them correctly. It is recommended that you practise them first on your own hands – or feet if you can reach them. In a comprehensive reflexology treatment, like the one set out in Part Two, you will use five basic pressure-point techniques. These are: thumb-walking, finger-walking, pivoting, sliding and pinching. The same techniques can be used on both the feet and the hands.

In general, the amount of pressure exerted when using any of these techniques should be adjusted to the person you are treating. A firmer pressure would be used on a strong adult than would be used on a frail or elderly person, or a child. If you notice that the veins on the top or side of the foot, or the back of the hands, are pronounced, make sure that you use only very gentle pressure, to avoid the risk of causing a haematoma (bruise) – an accumulation of blood under the skin from vessels injured by a blow or disease.

Each technique is adapted to the particular reflex it is treating. Thumb-walking is used on the majority of reflexes found on the hands and feet, with the exception of the very small points. As the name suggests, the thumb literally walks lightly over the surface of the skin. Finger-walking is a similar technique, but employs one or more of the fingers. Pivoting is the technique used on small reflex points – for instance, the pituitary gland found in the centre of the big toe: the tip of the thumb is rotated slowly on the reflex.

The remaining two techniques are used less frequently, but can nonetheless be useful for particular problems. Sliding, for example, can help break down crystal deposits. As the name suggests, it is performed by sliding the thumb over an area while maintaining a gentle pressure. This technique is used mostly on the soles of the feet and the palms of the hands as it is a fairly robust action. The tops of the feet and the backs of the hands are more delicate and this type of pressure could be painful. Pinching is a technique used on hands or feet only to treat lymph drainage.

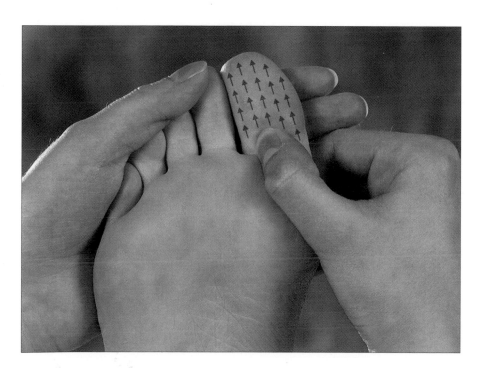

**Thumb-walking** With the thumb bent at the first joint, and only the outer edge of the tip of the thumb in contact with the foot, take tiny 'steps' all over the reflex being worked – here, the back of the head. It is important that the thumb is constantly kept bent, and not continually flexed and straightened as it walks forward, as this could cause problems in the joint. When you place your thumb on the foot, make sure that it is positioned in a way that allows the flesh of the outer edge of the thumb to fold in towards the nail. This prevents the nail being pressed into the foot.

Try practising thumb-walking on your own hands *(far right)*. Bend your thumb and place the outer edge, with the flesh folded in towards the nail, onto the palm of your hand. Place the other four fingers against the back of the treated hand for support, before applying pressure. Make sure that the pressure is applied only by the thumb and not by the fingers – these are acting merely as a buffer against the pressure. After you have pressed your thumb into your hand, pull back to relieve the pressure but without losing contact. Then take one small step forward, press and pull back. Continue to do this across and up the palm of your hand.

When you first work with thumb-walking you may find that your hands become very tired. This will improve as your muscles become stronger through practise.

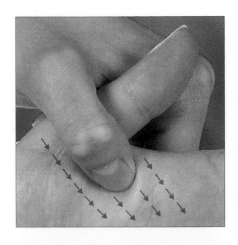

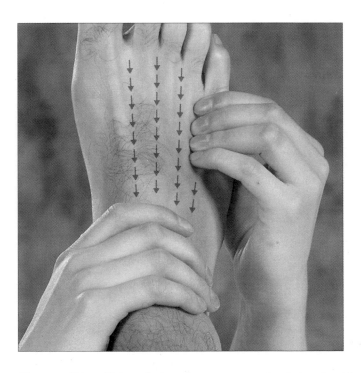

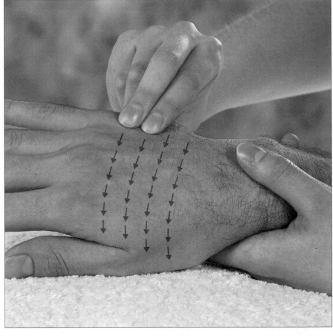

**Finger-walking** This technique is applied mainly to the top and sides of the feet *(above)* and the back of the hands. Depending on which reflex is being worked, either one, two or all four fingers can be used. To treat the lymphatic system, for example, place the tips of all four bent fingers of your working hand on the top of the foot, close to the little toe, and your working thumb on the sole of the foot for support. Gently pressing and pulling back, walk all four fingers together down the top of the foot. Two-finger-walking *(above right)* is often used to treat reflexes on the back of the hand. Wrap your supporting hand around the patient's wrist. Place your index and middle fingers on the lateral side of the patient's hand, with your working thumb on the palm for support. Starting at the little finger's web, walk down the back of the hand across the metacarpal bones until you reach the web between the thumb and index finger. Try this technique on your own hands.

**Pivoting** The position of the thumb and fingers is the same as for thumb-walking *(right)*. Use the outer edge of the thumb, so that the skin overlaps the nail, as before. Press on the point you wish to treat and slowly and gently pivot on it, keeping your thumb in contact, with the foot.

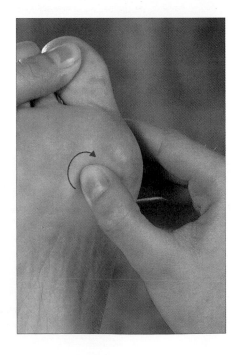

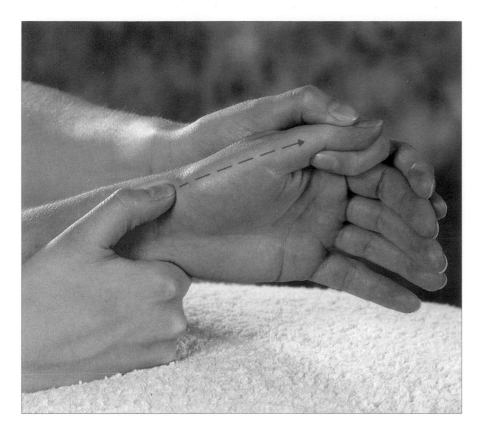

**Sliding** Adopt the same thumb and finger positions as for thumb-walking. Press your working thumb gently into the foot or hand *(left)* and, maintaining the pressure, gently slide it along 1.25 cm (½ in). Pull your thumb back slightly before sliding along another 1.25 cm (½ in). Continue in this way until you have covered the reflex with which you are working. To treat the spinal reflex on the hand, for example, first thumb-walk along the reflex, down the medial border of the hand to the wrist. Then change over hands and, with the fingers of your working hand placed on the back of the patient's hand for support and holding the patient's thumb, slide your working thumb 1.25 cm (½ in) back up the reflex. Take your thumb back slightly, and slide up a further 1.25 cm (½ in). Continue this movement until you reach the base of the thumb nail.

# Massage techniques

Massage on the feet or hands can be used prior to treatment to relax patients who are tense or under stress, and to stimulate energy after treatment has been completed. There are five basic techniques: wringing, kneading, stretching, finger circling and stroking. These techniques are most effective when performed in this order.

Wringing helps to smooth out the feet or hands by stretching the muscles. It is followed by kneading, which relaxes the person and stimulates body energy.

Stretching literally stretches the muscles, allowing the bones more freedom of movement. When performed on the feet, it makes the whole body feel as if it were being pulled upwards. It actually helps to elongate feet that have been cramped up in tight shoes all day, or hands that have been clenched or storing tension.

Finger circling, used on either the feet or the hands, is a wonderful movement for relaxing a person. If your patient is very tense, this can be carried out on either feet or hands – depending on which you are treating – before starting the actual treatment.

Stroking can be a very soothing movement, wonderful for removing tension.

All of these techniques can be used on both the feet and the hands. Just as with the pressure-point techniques, adjust the pressure according to the person you are treating. To make sure your hands are quite smooth and dry, apply a small amount of talcum powder to them before massaging. You will find that they move over your patient's feet and hands much more easily.

Again, it is useful to practise the techniques on yourself before you attempt to massage another person.

**Wringing** Beginning at the top of the foot near the toes *(below)*, wrap your hands around the sides of the foot, with the thumbs on the sole and the fingers on the top of the foot. Gently twist your hands back and forth in a wringing action *(below right)* as you move down the foot towards the ankle. This is most beneficial for people who encase their feet in tight shoes, because the action of the hands stretches out the feet. To massage the hands, use the same action, with your hands in a similar position as for the feet. It is impossible to practise this stroke on your own hands since you need to use both of them, but if you can reach your feet easily, it is helpful to practise on them.

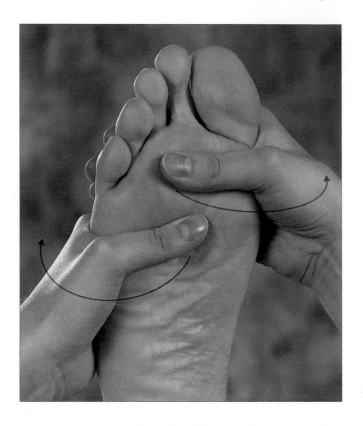

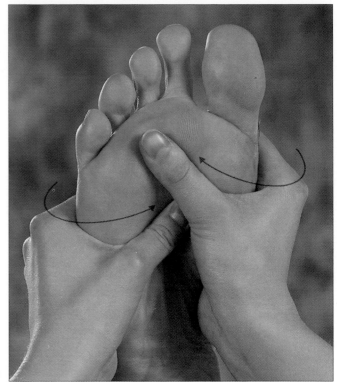

**Kneading** Place one hand across the top of the foot and place the clenched fist of the other hand on the sole of the foot *(right)*. Pressing both hands into the feet, make circular movements with both hands over the entire foot.

To massage the hands, place one hand across the back of your patient's hand, and place the clenched fist of your other hand on the palm. Make circular movements with both your hands while applying pressure over the entire surface of the hand.

Again, this is impossible to practise on your own hands, but try it out on your feet if you can.

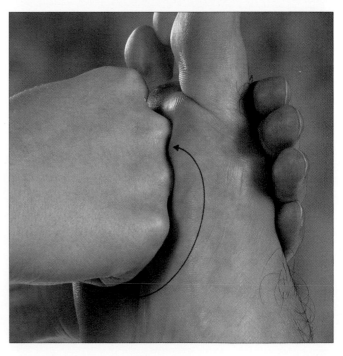

**Stretching** The position of the hands on the foot *(below)* is the same as for the wringing action. Starting near the ankle, pull your hands up towards the toes. Repeat several times. Do the same for the hands *(below right)*. Starting near the wrists, pull the hands towards the fingers. Repeat several times. The effect of this massage is to stretch the foot or the hand.

During the course of a day, through the pull of gravity, the body has a tendency to shrink by a couple of centimetres (an inch or so). How many of you who drive adjust your rearview mirror in the morning, and then have to readjust it in the evening?

Since it is not possible to practise this technique on your own hands, practise on your feet if you can.

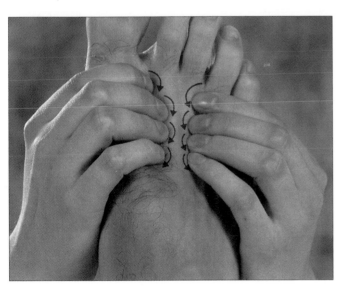

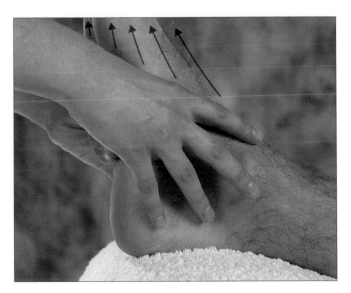

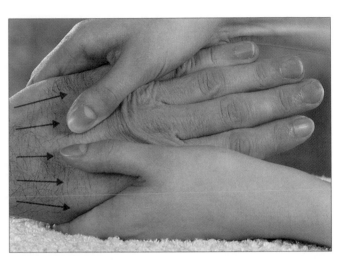

**Finger circling** When treating the feet *(above)*, place the fingers of both your hands on top of your patient's foot, and your thumbs on the sole for support. Gently make tiny circular movements with your fingers over the top and side of the foot, and over the ankle bones.

For the hands, start at the base of the fingers on the back of the hand, and use a finger circling action towards and around the wrist.

**Stroking** For the feet, start at the ankle *(above)* and allow the fingers of both hands to gently stroke the top and sides of the foot in an upward movement towards the toes. This can be maintained for as long as you think it necessary.

For the hands, start at the wrists and gently stroke the back and sides in an upward movement towards the fingers. On the hands too, maintain this for the time you feel is right.

# Giving a reflexology treatment

Ideally, a reflexology treatment should be given in comfortable and pleasant surroundings: a place which promotes peace and relaxation. This is important for both those giving and receiving treatment. Each treatment should last for about one hour – less on children because they have smaller feet. The minimum time lapse between treatments can be three days; for the majority of people, treatment is given at weekly intervals. This gives the body time to eliminate the toxins that reflexology has activated and to adjust to a new level of energy.

If it is your client's first treatment, he or she may not know what to expect and could be apprehensive. This is why it is advisable to explain what you are going to do before you do it. Tell your client that if pain is experienced on pressure you must be told, because this indicates a blockage of energy in that part of the body which relates to the reflex zone being worked. Give some warning of possible side effects, such as a feeling of tiredness, increased sweating and perhaps having to visit the lavatory more often; and that a condition can sometimes,become worse before getting better. If this is not explained to a client, it can be very alarming.

Always enquire into your client's medical history. This can provide insight into present problems. If the person you have chosen to treat is taking medication, on no account suggest that it be interrupted: certain drugs can produce severe withdrawal symptoms, and if you are not aware of this you could create problems for the person concerned. A client's medication should only be stopped by the doctor – or whoever prescribed it.

If your client complains of pains, or describes any other symptoms to you, always ask if they have had it checked medically. If they have not, then suggest that they do so. As reflexologists, we are not allowed to make a medical diagnosis. We may suspect that a person is suffering from a certain ailment, but we are not allowed to say so. We are only allowed to describe it as an energy imbalance.

After gleaning all the necessary information, seat your client so that the feet are at a comfortable height for you to treat. Have a box of tissues handy. If someone has travelled a long way or has come straight from work, you may feel that the feet need washing.

Above *Fresh and peaceful surroundings are essential for a successful treatment.*

Never be embarrassed to ask your clients to do this. In my experience, they are only too happy to oblige.

Prior to starting the actual treatment, it is important to make a visual observation of the feet and/or hands, because these can supply important information. Start with the skeletal structure. Changes in this could indicate a disturbance in the energy flow within the reflex zone, resulting in a disorder in the corresponding part of the body. One example is feet that have bunions. These affect the reflex zones to the cervical spine and thyroid gland.

Look at the colour and state of the skin. Swelling in the feet could relate to congestion in the corresponding part of the body. If the swelling is around the ankle, it could indicate a kidney, a heart or a circulatory disorder. Another sign of heart and circulatory disorders is the presence of tiny pads around the base of the toes on the front of the left foot. Notice also the condition of the skin.

Calluses and corns could point to problems in the body related to the zone that they cover. A corn on the outer side of the small toe, for example, could reflect an injury to the shoulder; a corn on the pad of one or more of the toes could mirror sinus problems. See whether the skin is excessively dry. This could either be a sign of poor circulation in the outer extremities of the body, or it could refer to a hormonal imbalance. If the feet have been neglected and are covered in rough, hard skin, it would be expedient to suggest a visit to a chiropodist to have this removed.

Finally, look at the nails on the feet and hands. As explained earlier in this section, these can reveal a great deal about a person's health. If, for example, you find that the nail bed appears to be rather pale and you suspect anaemia, suggest a visit to a doctor.

Once you have completed your visual observations, the moment is right to begin your reflexology treatment.

## Caution

A few points are worth bearing in mind before starting the treatment.

1. It is preferable not to give any treatment in the presence of certain disorders unless you are a fully qualified reflexologist. Among them can be included the following: osteoporosis, arthritis in the feet or hands, certain heart conditions such as thrombosis and phlebitis, diabetes, and pregnancy – especially during the first sixteen weeks if there is a history of a miscarriage.
2. Treatment should not be given to cancer patients undergoing chemotherapy, radium or hormonal treatment unless you are a fully qualified reflexologist.
3. Complete treatment does not necessarily include both the hands and the feet. Treat the hands when the feet are not in good condition, and vice versa. For example, if the person you are about to treat suffers from athlete's foot or verrucas, make sure you treat the hands only, until the foot condition has cleared.
4. Lastly, if you are not a qualified reflexologist, or in any doubt about giving a treatment, always seek professional advice before you start.

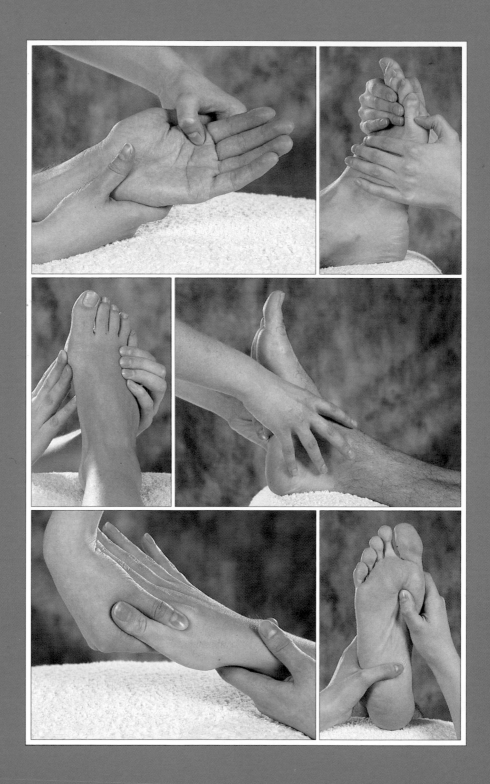

# 2

# The step-by-step treatment

This part of the book guides you, step by step, through a complete reflexology treatment. It is important to remember that the whole of the right foot must be treated before you move on to treat the left foot. The same applies if you are working on the hands. Colour photographs, with inset line drawings showing the transverse lines and highlighting the reflex area or point to work on, and detailed captions, demonstrate clearly how to carry out the treatment. Charts pertaining to all aspects of both feet and hands are given at the beginning of this section. Study them prior to starting your treatment. Familiarize yourself with the positions of the longitudinal zones, the transverse zones and the diaphragm. It will help you to locate the reflexes accurately. Some of them are only the size of a pinhead and may initially be difficult to find, but with practice you will learn to feel those points.

The anatomy and physiology of the body and relating reflexes are described. It is very important to study this. Since you are treating the whole body, you need to be acquainted with its different systems; how they function individually and in relation to each other; and the various disorders associated with each one. Patients who seek a reflexology treatment understandably expect the therapist to know about the organs of the body and their function.

Before you start a treatment, discuss what you intend to do with your patient. Holistic therapies treat the cause of the disease, not the symptom; and in order to find the *cause* you must encourage patients to talk. But remember the two golden rules: be a good listener; and never repeat anything said to you by your patient in confidence.

Opposite *Using special pressure-point and massage techniques, reflexology is able to detect and dissipate energy blocks reflected on the feet and the hands. In this way it helps the body to heal itself.*

# The reflex areas on the feet

This and the following charts indicate the position of every reflex on the feet, and the part of the body to which it relates.

Reflex areas are found on the sole, the top, the medial (inner) and the lateral (outer) sides of both feet. Reflexes to the organs situated

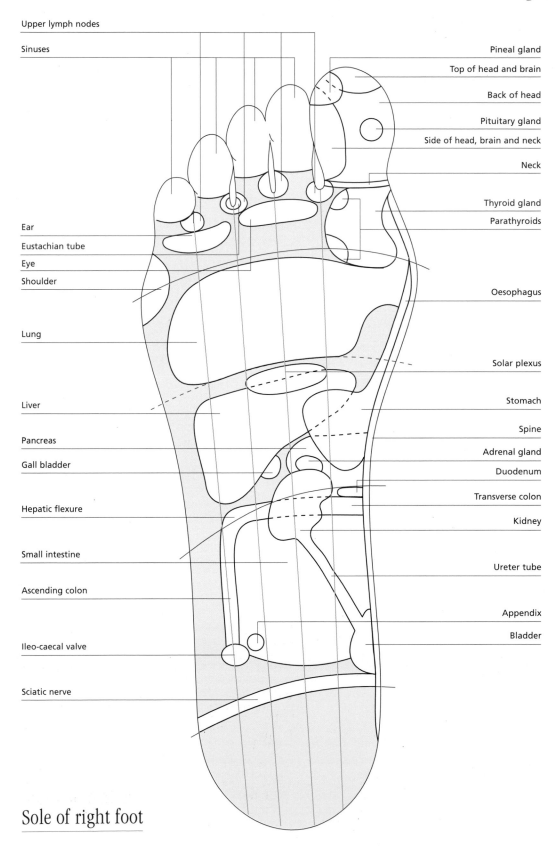

Upper lymph nodes

Sinuses

Ear

Eustachian tube

Eye

Shoulder

Lung

Liver

Pancreas

Gall bladder

Hepatic flexure

Small intestine

Ascending colon

Ileo-caecal valve

Sciatic nerve

Pineal gland

Top of head and brain

Back of head

Pituitary gland

Side of head, brain and neck

Neck

Thyroid gland

Parathyroids

Oesophagus

Solar plexus

Stomach

Spine

Adrenal gland

Duodenum

Transverse colon

Kidney

Ureter tube

Appendix

Bladder

## Sole of right foot

on the right side of the body are found on the right foot; those situated on the left side are found on the left foot. Note that some reflexes are located on one foot only. For example, the liver reflex lies on the right foot only; the heart reflex lies on the left foot only, and so on. Some organs are distributed across both feet. Before starting your treatment, study these charts carefully to help you locate the reflexes accurately. For further guidance, the transverse and longitudinal zones are indicated, as well as the diaphragm (dotted line).

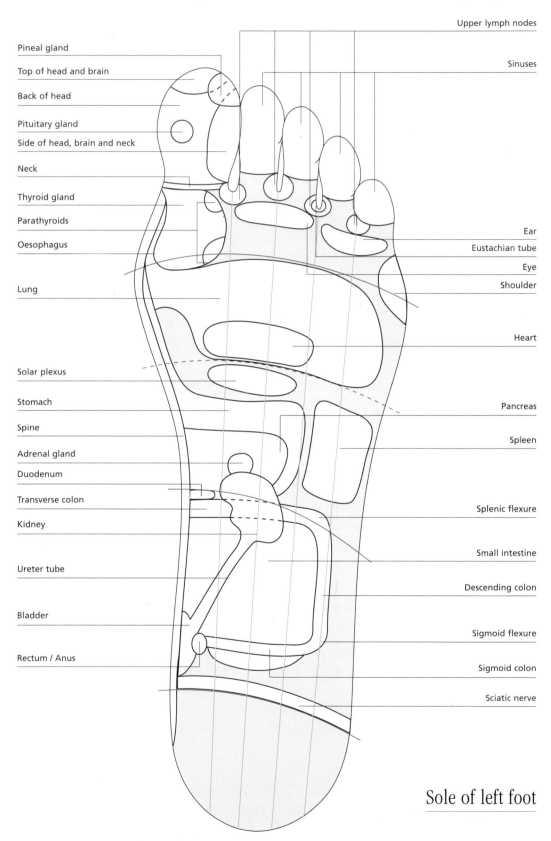

Pineal gland
Top of head and brain
Back of head
Pituitary gland
Side of head, brain and neck
Neck
Thyroid gland
Parathyroids
Oesophagus
Lung
Solar plexus
Stomach
Spine
Adrenal gland
Duodenum
Transverse colon
Kidney
Ureter tube
Bladder
Rectum / Anus

Upper lymph nodes
Sinuses
Ear
Eustachian tube
Eye
Shoulder
Heart
Pancreas
Spleen
Splenic flexure
Small intestine
Descending colon
Sigmoid flexure
Sigmoid colon
Sciatic nerve

## Sole of left foot

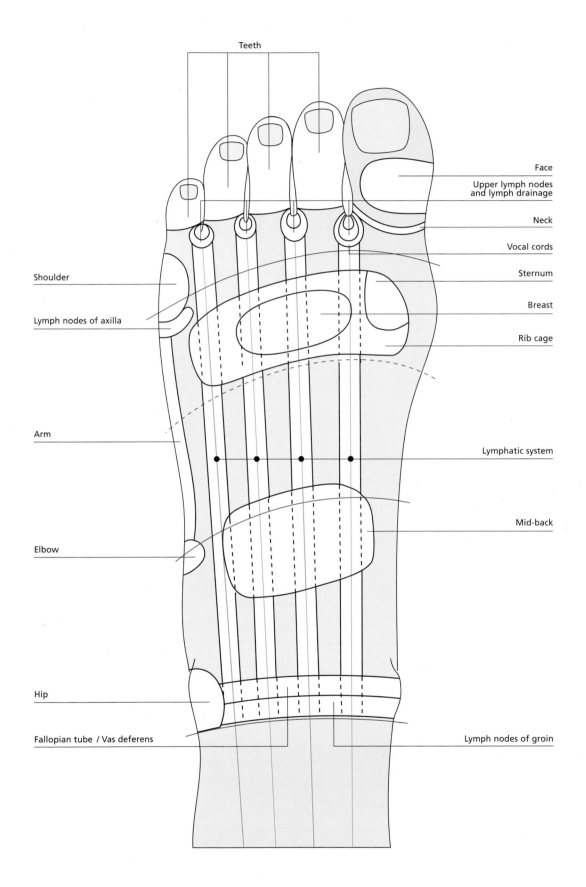

Teeth

Face

Upper lymph nodes
and lymph drainage

Neck

Vocal cords

Shoulder

Sternum

Lymph nodes of axilla

Breast

Rib cage

Arm

Lymphatic system

Elbow

Mid-back

Hip

Fallopian tube / Vas deferens

Lymph nodes of groin

## Top of left foot

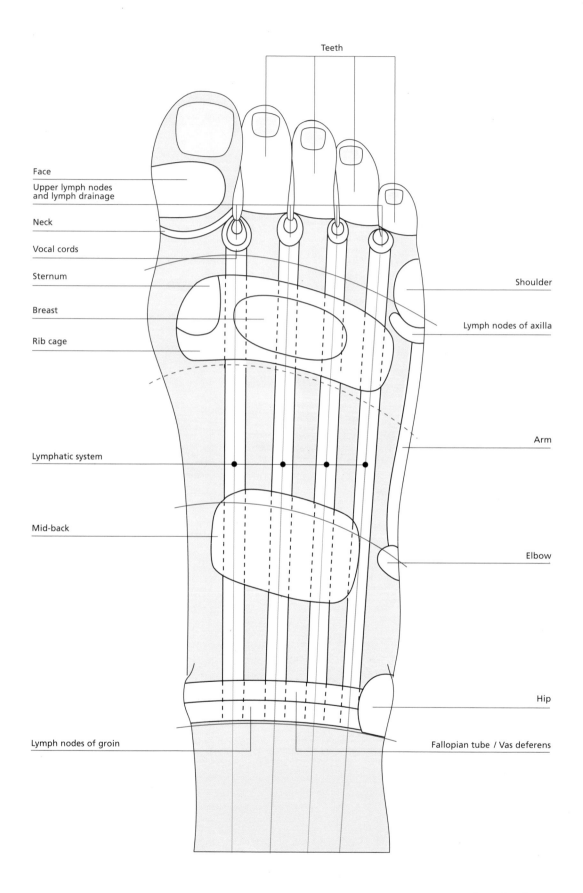

Teeth

Face

Upper lymph nodes
and lymph drainage

Neck

Vocal cords

Sternum

Breast

Rib cage

Shoulder

Lymph nodes of axilla

Lymphatic system

Arm

Mid-back

Elbow

Hip

Lymph nodes of groin

Fallopian tube / Vas deferens

Top of right foot

# Medial and lateral sides of right foot

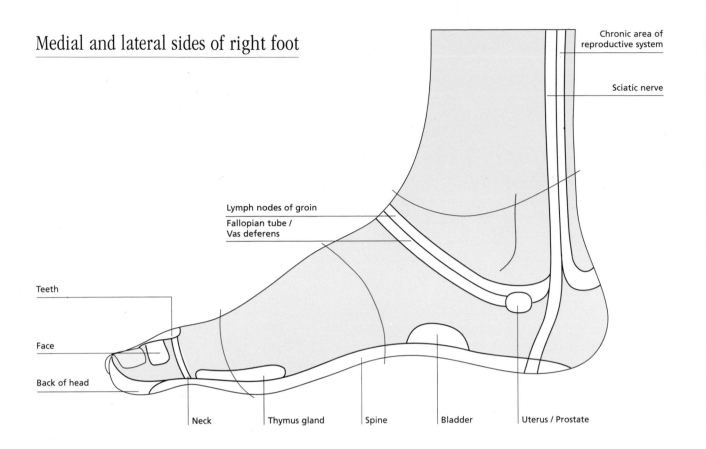

Chronic area of reproductive system

Sciatic nerve

Lymph nodes of groin

Fallopian tube / Vas deferens

Teeth

Face

Back of head

Neck

Thymus gland

Spine

Bladder

Uterus / Prostate

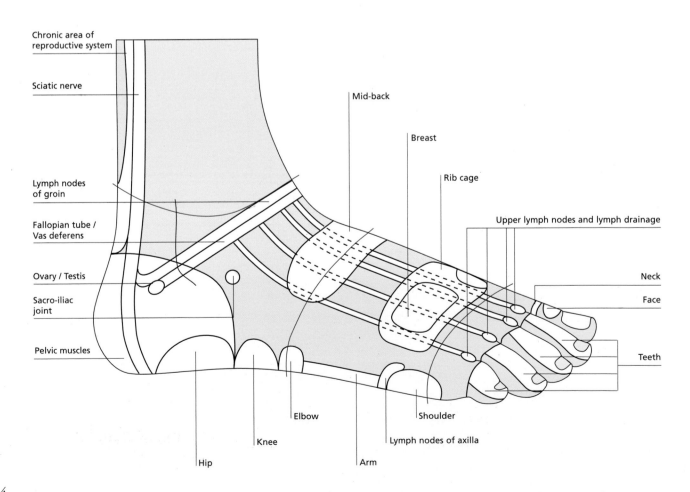

Chronic area of reproductive system

Sciatic nerve

Lymph nodes of groin

Fallopian tube / Vas deferens

Ovary / Testis

Sacro-iliac joint

Pelvic muscles

Mid-back

Breast

Rib cage

Upper lymph nodes and lymph drainage

Neck

Face

Teeth

Hip

Knee

Elbow

Arm

Shoulder

Lymph nodes of axilla

## Medial and lateral sides of left foot

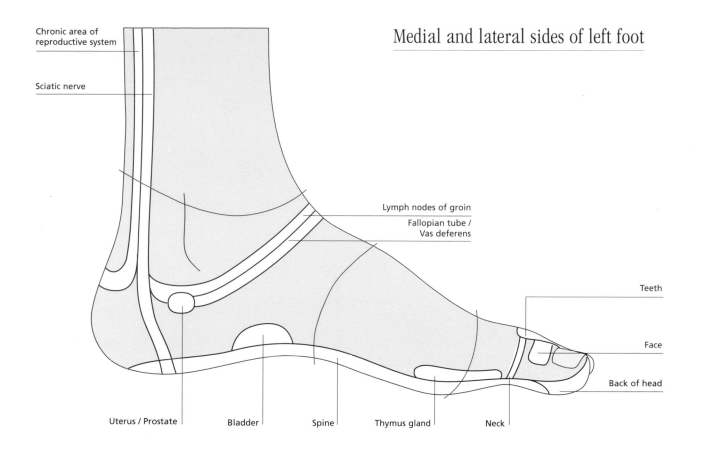

Chronic area of reproductive system

Sciatic nerve

Lymph nodes of groin

Fallopian tube / Vas deferens

Teeth

Face

Back of head

Uterus / Prostate

Bladder

Spine

Thymus gland

Neck

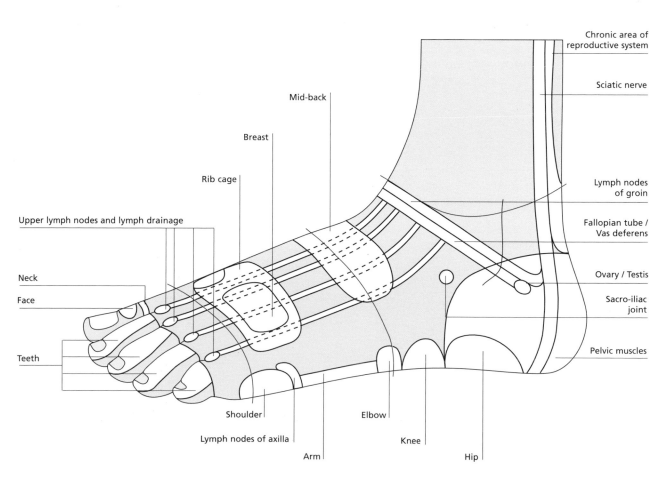

Mid-back

Breast

Rib cage

Upper lymph nodes and lymph drainage

Neck

Face

Teeth

Shoulder

Lymph nodes of axilla

Arm

Elbow

Knee

Hip

Chronic area of reproductive system

Sciatic nerve

Lymph nodes of groin

Fallopian tube / Vas deferens

Ovary / Testis

Sacro-iliac joint

Pelvic muscles

35

# The reflex areas on the hands

Similar reflexes exist on the hands as on the feet, but the reflex areas are smaller because the hands present a smaller area to be treated. These reflex areas are found on the palm, the top, the medial (inner) and the lateral (outer) sides of both hands. As in the feet, organs of

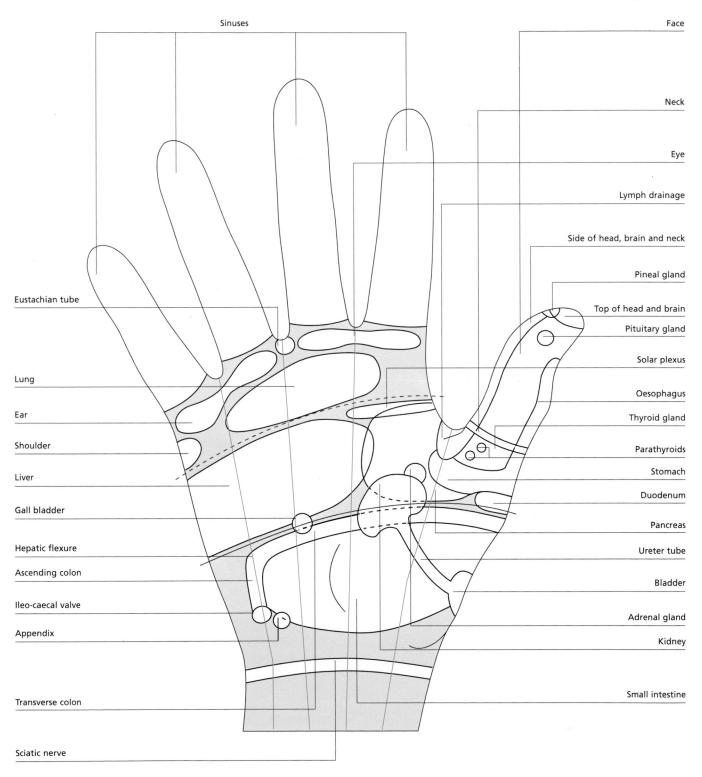

Sinuses

Face

Neck

Eye

Lymph drainage

Side of head, brain and neck

Pineal gland

Eustachian tube

Top of head and brain

Pituitary gland

Solar plexus

Lung

Oesophagus

Ear

Thyroid gland

Shoulder

Parathyroids

Liver

Stomach

Duodenum

Gall bladder

Pancreas

Hepatic flexure

Ureter tube

Ascending colon

Bladder

Ileo-caecal valve

Adrenal gland

Appendix

Kidney

Transverse colon

Small intestine

Sciatic nerve

Palm of right hand

36

the body located in a particular zone will have corresponding reflexes in the same zone on the hands. The right hand relates to the organs on the right side of the body; the left hand relates to organs on the left side of the body. For example, the liver reflex is found only on the right hand; the heart reflex is found only on the left hand. Study these charts carefully before you start treatment. For further guidance, the transverse zones and the longitudinal zones are indicated. as well as the diaphragm (dotted line).

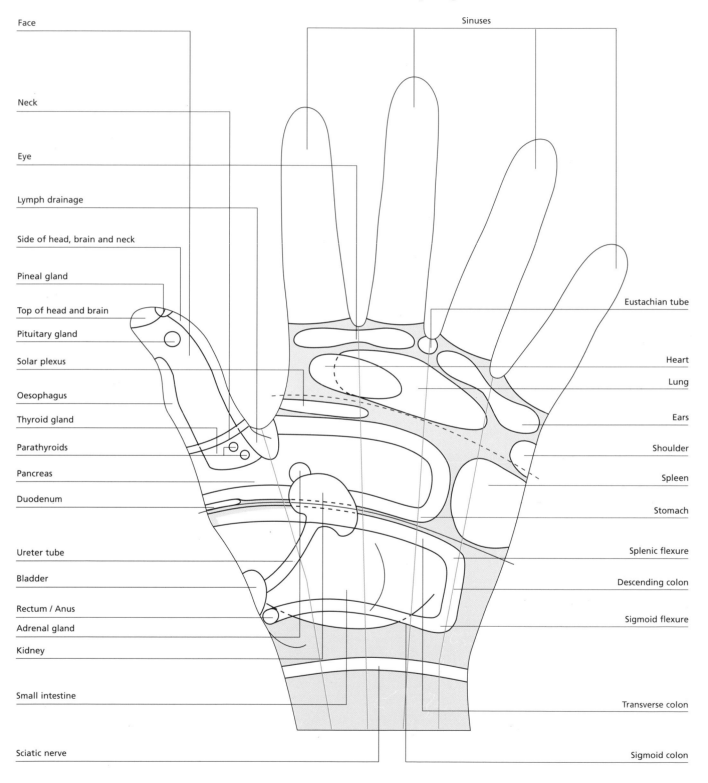

Face

Neck

Eye

Lymph drainage

Side of head, brain and neck

Pineal gland

Top of head and brain

Pituitary gland

Solar plexus

Oesophagus

Thyroid gland

Parathyroids

Pancreas

Duodenum

Ureter tube

Bladder

Rectum / Anus

Adrenal gland

Kidney

Small intestine

Sciatic nerve

Sinuses

Eustachian tube

Heart

Lung

Ears

Shoulder

Spleen

Stomach

Splenic flexure

Descending colon

Sigmoid flexure

Transverse colon

Sigmoid colon

## Palm of left hand

# Back of left hand

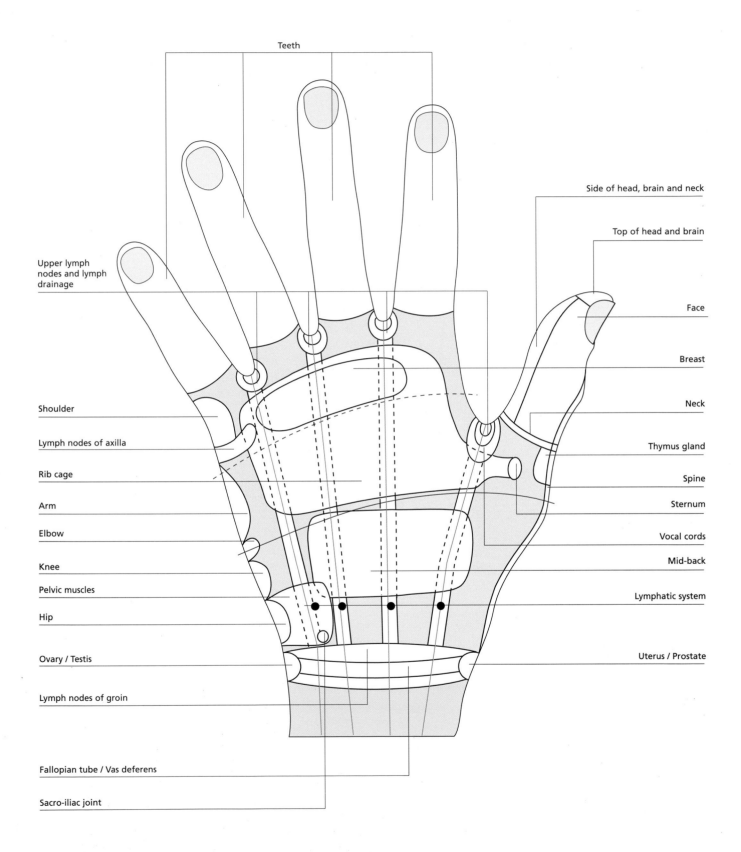

Teeth

Side of head, brain and neck

Top of head and brain

Upper lymph nodes and lymph drainage

Face

Breast

Neck

Shoulder

Thymus gland

Lymph nodes of axilla

Spine

Rib cage

Sternum

Arm

Vocal cords

Elbow

Mid-back

Knee

Pelvic muscles

Lymphatic system

Hip

Ovary / Testis

Uterus / Prostate

Lymph nodes of groin

Fallopian tube / Vas deferens

Sacro-iliac joint

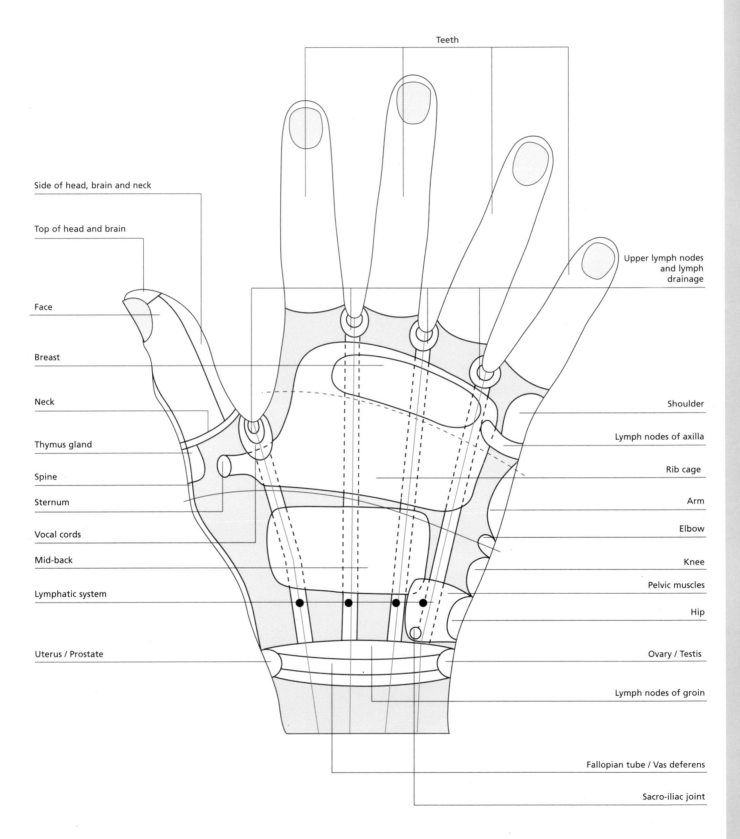

Teeth

Side of head, brain and neck

Top of head and brain

Face

Breast

Neck

Thymus gland

Spine

Sternum

Vocal cords

Mid-back

Lymphatic system

Uterus / Prostate

Upper lymph nodes and lymph drainage

Shoulder

Lymph nodes of axilla

Rib cage

Arm

Elbow

Knee

Pelvic muscles

Hip

Ovary / Testis

Lymph nodes of groin

Fallopian tube / Vas deferens

Sacro-iliac joint

# Beginning the treatment

A reflexology treatment works towards an unrestricted flow of energy throughout the physical body. An uncomfortable seat or posture can create tension that impedes this energy flow. When choosing a position, it is important to ensure that it affords complete relaxation. If you are treating the feet, the ideal one allows the feet to be raised to a suitable height for treatment, the knees slightly bent to alleviate tension in the calf and thigh muscles, and the trunk of the body positioned at such an angle that the patient's face is visible to the therapist: facial expressions impart important information.

Rotation of the ankles and wrists, and toes and fingers, helps to alleviate stiffness in the joints and aids the release of any energy blocks. Note that it is considered bad practice to allow the patient's feet – or hands – to be supported on the therapist's lap.

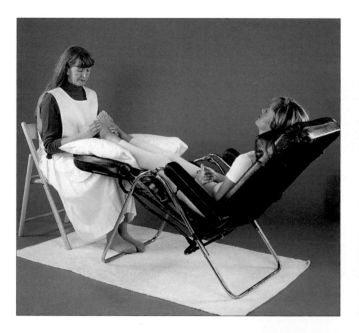

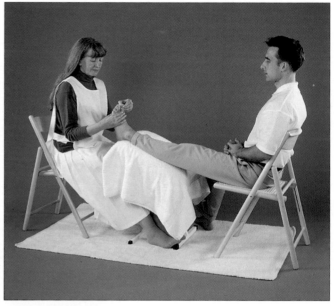

A reflexology or recliner chair *(above)* is ideal for treatment. The body is positioned at the correct angle and achieves complete relaxation. It also provides a comfortable position for the therapist to work from. For further patient comfort, pillows can be placed under the head and beneath the legs and feet. A disposable towel should be used to cover the pillows, and renewed for each patient.

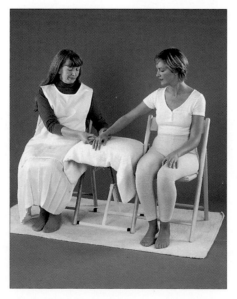

If you are unable to purchase a recliner chair, a reflexology stool can be used *(above)*. Adjustable in height, it has a footrest that can be tilted at varying angles to allow the best position of the patient's legs and feet.

The reflexology stool is ideal when treating hands *(left)*. The easiest position for this is to sit alongside your patient with the stool between you. Cover the stool with a towel over which is placed a disposable towel. Make sure that the stool is the correct height to afford a comfortable treatment for both your patient and you, the therapist.

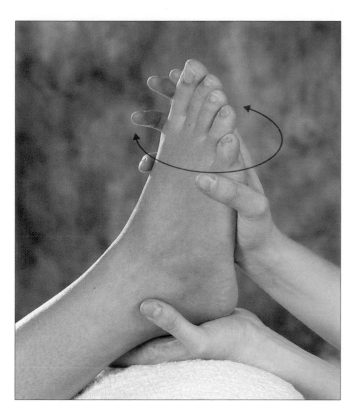

When using rotation *(left)*, exercise caution, especially if you are treating someone who is frail or has an arthritic condition. Start with the right foot or hand, rotating first the ankle or wrist and then the toes or fingers. Support the foot by placing one hand at the back of the heel. Your thumb and first two fingers rest on either side of the ankle joint. Your working hand holds the foot and slowly rotates the ankle.

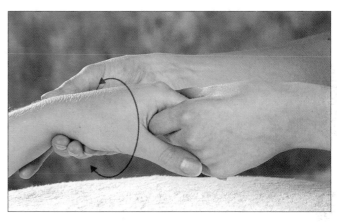

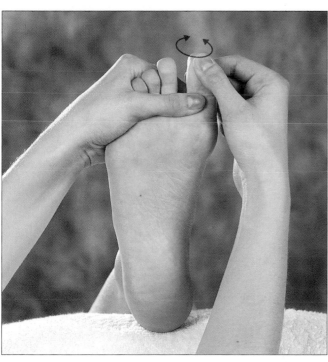

When you have treated the ankle, move your supporting hand to the top of the foot *(above)*. With your working hand slowly rotate each toe, holding it by its middle joint. Work in both a clockwise and anticlockwise direction.

Support the patient's hand *(top)* with your thumb and two fingers on either side of the wrist joint. With your working hand, slowly rotate your patient's wrist. Then support the patient's knuckles *(above)* while your working hand slowly rotates fingers and thumb in turn, holding each at the middle joint.

# Head and neck reflexes

The reflexes relating to the head and the neck are located on the five toes and five fingers of both feet and both hands. Each big toe and thumb can be divided into five longitudinal zones corresponding to the head and brain area. All the reflexes pertaining to the head and neck are found in the first transverse zone which covers the phalanges, ending at the metatarsals on the feet and the metacarpals on the hands. Treatment should start with the pituitary gland and continue in the sequence given in the step-by-step guide. Working methodically in this way will ensure that none of the reflexes are overlooked.

## Pituitary gland

This gland lies at the base of the brain, just above and behind the nasal cavity. It is only the size of a pea and is the master gland of the endocrine system. The pituitary gland consists of an anterior and a posterior lobe which have different functions. The anterior

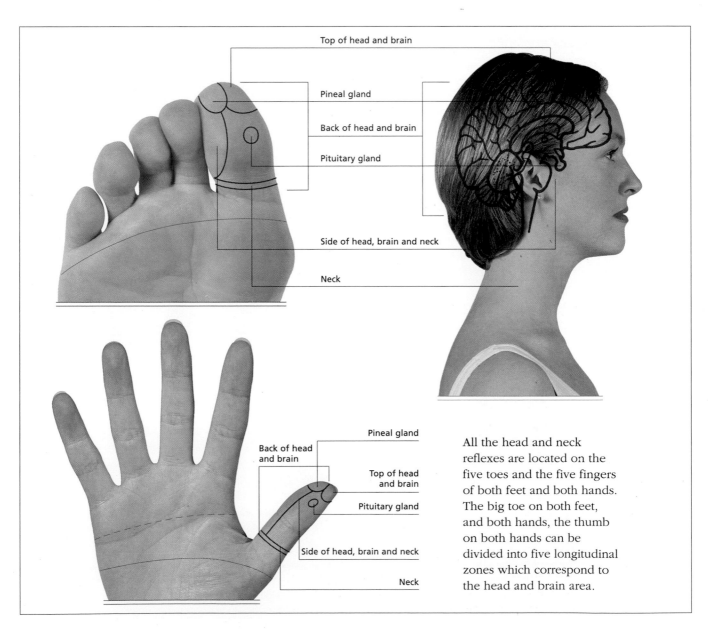

Top of head and brain

Pineal gland

Back of head and brain

Pituitary gland

Side of head, brain and neck

Neck

Pineal gland

Back of head and brain

Top of head and brain

Pituitary gland

Side of head, brain and neck

Neck

All the head and neck reflexes are located on the five toes and the five fingers of both feet and both hands. The big toe on both feet, and both hands, the thumb on both hands can be divided into five longitudinal zones which correspond to the head and brain area.

42

lobe produces hormones which stimulate the thyroid and adrenal glands, affect sexual life and govern the secretion of breast milk. The posterior lobe secretes hormones that stimulate the muscles of the uterus during and after childbirth, stimulate the breasts to produce milk, cause the contraction of involuntary muscles and act as an antidiuretic. This reflex area is important for hormonal imbalances.

### Pineal gland

The pineal gland is approximately the same size as the pituitary gland and is situated just in front of the cerebellum which lies low down at the back of the skull. Its principal function is to secrete melatonin which affects the body's biological clock. If the level of this hormone in the blood is too high during daylight hours, it produces a condition known as seasonal affective disorder (or SAD). This gland also regulates the onset of puberty, induces sleep and influences our moods.

### Head and brain

The head, containing the brain, controls and monitors all bodily functions. The brain is a soft jelly-like structure made up of about 1,000 billion neurons, and is one of the largest organs of the body. It is divided into four principle parts: the diencephalon, the cerebrum, the cerebellum, and the brain stem which is a continuation of the spinal cord. The cerebellum is responsible for coordinating reflex actions, controlling posture, balance and muscular activity. The cerebrum contains the nerve centres responsible for conscious thought and action. This reflex is important for conditions such as headaches, migraine, Parkinson's disease, epilepsy, cerebral palsy, multiple sclerosis, trigeminal neuralgia (or tic douloureux) and dyslexia.

### Vertebral column (spine)

The vertebral column is made up of thirty-three vertebrae. These are divided into seven cervical vertebrae (in the neck region), twelve thoracic (posterior to the thoracic cavity), five lumbar (in charge of supporting the lower back), five sacral, which are fused into one bone to form the sacrum, and four which are fused into either one or two bones to form the coccyx. The vertebral column encloses and protects the spinal cord, supports the head and serves as a point of attachment for the ribs and muscles of the back. Treatment to this reflex is advised for back pain, and for diseases associated with the spinal nerves.

### Neck

The reflex to the neck is found around the base of the big toe and thumb, a third of the way along the lateral border. Gentle rotation of the big toes or thumbs can alleviate tension in the neck. If the thumb or toe joints are stiff, it may indicate rigidity in this area.

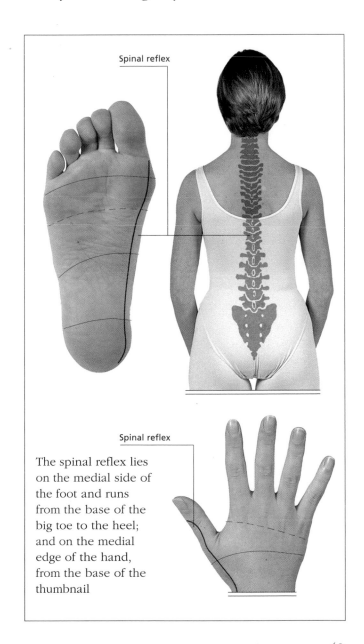

Spinal reflex

Spinal reflex

The spinal reflex lies on the medial side of the foot and runs from the base of the big toe to the heel; and on the medial edge of the hand, from the base of the thumbnail

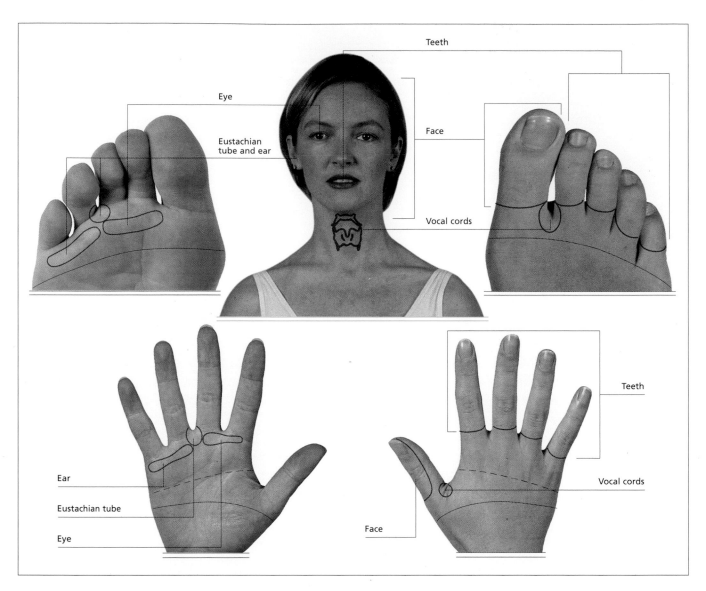

## Face

The reflex to the face, like the reflex to the back of the head, can be divided into five longitudinal zones. The right foot or hand represents the right side of the face and the left foot or hand, the left side. All parts of the face, such as the eyes, nose, sinuses, teeth, lips and muscles are included in this reflex. Problems related to the face such as sinusitis, toothache, eye strain and Bell's palsy (facial paralysis) can be helped through this reflex.

## Vocal cords

The larynx is a complicated cartilagenous structure lying between the pharynx and the trachea. Running inside the larynx are two membranes known as the vocal cords. Using these membranes for voice production is a highly complex operation of coordination between the breath, the lips, the tongue and the vocal cords. This is an important reflex in cases of laryngitis, pharyngitis and tracheitis.

## Sinuses

The sinuses are cavities in the bones of the face and skull which are linked by narrow channels to the nose. They are situated in the forehead just above the eyes, in the cheek-bones, and between and behind the eyes. The sinuses lighten the skull bones and serve as resonant sound chambers when we speak or sing. They are lined with a membrane that secretes mucus which drains into the nose to be cleared. Inflammation of the sinuses can be caused by a viral infection, or a swelling of the mucous membranes associated with hay

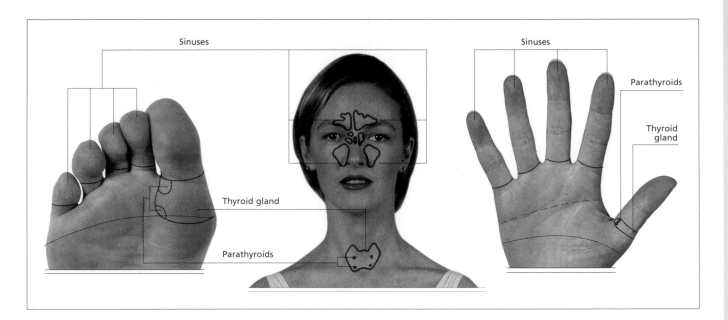

fever. These reflexes are important in the treatment of colds, catarrh and hay fever.

### Eyes

The eyes are the complicated and extremely efficient organs of vision. Set in their bony sockets, they are protected from injury. Self-focusing, self-lubricating and self-cleansing, they adapt to bright or dim light and to distant or near vision. This reflex is important for eye strain, conjunctivitis, cataract and all other conditions related to the eyes.

### Ear and eustachian tube

Our hearing is one of the most sensitive and discriminating of senses. Sound is perceived by the brain. When sound waves fall on the eardrum, they cause it to vibrate. The vibrations reach the inner ear, causing the fluid in its cavity to vibrate in turn, thereby exciting nerve endings which carry the impulses to the brain. The eustachian tube starts at the back of the middle ear and opens into the throat. Its function is to equalize the pressure on either side of the eardrum. Both of these reflexes are important for conditions such as tinnitus, infections, deafness and vertigo.

### Thyroid gland

The thyroid gland has two lobes which are situated on either side of the windpipe, just below the level of the larynx. These lobes are joined by a narrow strip of thyroid tissue. The thyroid is unique among endocrine glands in that it requires iodine to make one of its two hormones, thyroxine. Its hormones affect the metabolism of practically all the tissues of the body: they regulate the rate at which oxygen is consumed, are powerful growth promoters, and are necessary for the full development of the brain. Treatment of this reflex is important for cretinism, myxedema, goiter and also imbalances in the reproductive glands.

### Parathyroid glands

These tiny glands, usually four in number, are superficially embedded in the back and side surfaces of each lobe of the thyroid. The hormone secreted by these glands is called parathormone, and is concerned with keeping a steady level of calcium and phosphorus in the blood. The parathyroid reflexes are helpful for cases of arthritis, osteoporosis, muscle twitching and spasms.

### Teeth

Every human has two sets of teeth. The first set of twenty primary teeth will usually have emerged by the age of three. By the age of twenty-five, the permanent set of thirty-two teeth have erupted. The reflexes for the teeth are important for conditions relating to dental problems, including abcesses, toothache and gingivitis – inflammation of the gums.

# Head and neck reflexes on the feet

These reflexes are all found in the first transverse zone and in all five longitudinal zones of the feet. When giving a reflexology treatment, always remember to work in a systematic order so as to avoid overlooking any of the reflex points. Start and complete treatment on the right foot before working with the left. As you work the reflexes, take note of any that are painful. Then return to these at the end of the session, so that you can give them extra treatment. If you feel that there may be something medically wrong with your patient, suggest that he or she visits a doctor for a check-up.

**1** Starting with the patient's right foot *(right)*, find **the pituitary gland reflex** in the centre of the fleshy pad of the big toe. If you have difficulty locating this point, try imagining a line crossing the big toe at the widest point, then imagine a vertical line down the centre of the toe. The pituitary reflex is found where these two lines cross. Support the foot with your left hand and support the front of the big toe with the fingers of your working hand. Press the reflex with the outer edge of your thumb, which should be slightly bent at the first joint. Make sure that your nail is not digging into the toe. Gently rotate on this point for a few seconds. This reflex can be very sensitive, so if your patient complains of pain, apply less pressure.

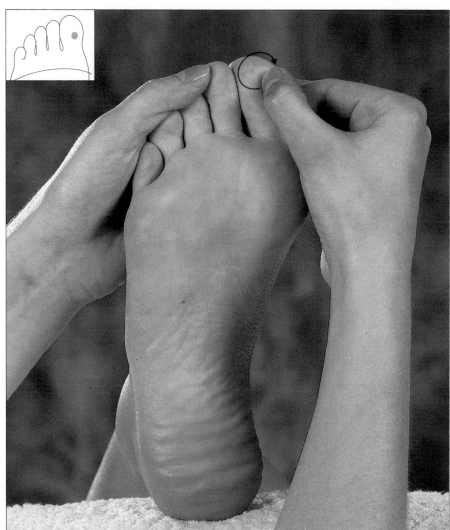

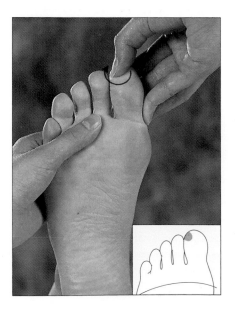

**2** Move the starting position of your thumb to the inner side of the big toe *(left)*, approximately 1.2 cm (½ in) down from the top. This is where the **pineal gland reflex** is located. Still supporting the foot with your left hand, approach this reflex with your working hand from above the foot. Use the fingers of your working hand to support the toe joint while you press the reflex with the outer edge of your bent thumb, and gently rotate on this point for a few seconds.

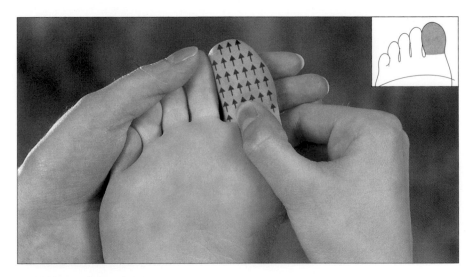

**3** After treating the pineal gland, move your working thumb to the lateral side of the foot, at the base of the big toe *(left)*. The **reflex for the back of the head** begins here, covering the whole of the fleshy pad on the toe. Support the foot with your left hand and the toe with the fingers of your working hand. Thumb-walk in six parallel lines from the base to the top of the toe.

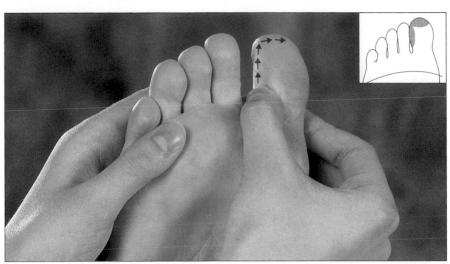

**4** To work the area relating to the **sides of the neck and head** and **the top of the brain** *(left)*, place your working thumb at the bottom of the lateral border of the big toe. Thumb-walk up the inside of the toe to the top of the toe. Change hands, using your other thumb to walk across the top of the toe.

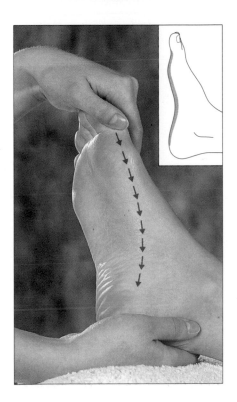
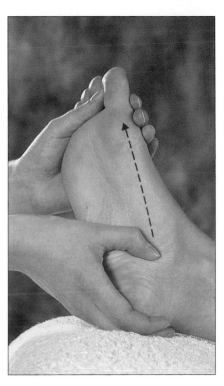

**5** Keep your working thumb on the medial edge at the top of the big toe. Support the foot under the heel with your right hand, tilting it slightly to the left *(far left)*. Now thumb-walk down the **spinal reflex**, which lies on the medial border of the big toe and the medial side of the foot, just below the arch, to two-thirds of the way along the calcaneum.

When you reach this point *(left)*, change hands and slide the outer edge of your right thumb back up the spinal reflex.

47

**6** To treat the **neck reflex**, position your thumb on the outer edge of the big toe *(below)*. Hold the front of the toes with your left hand and gently pull them back. Supporting the front of the big toe with your working-hand fingers, thumb-walk across the base of the toe.

**7** Without changing its position, use your working hand's first three fingers to walk across the **face reflex** *(below)* found on the front of the big toe. Your working thumb should support the back of the toe. This area includes reflexes for the eyes, nose, teeth, lips and facial muscles.

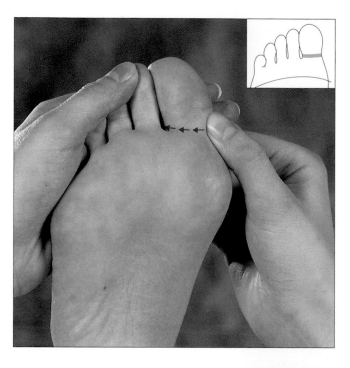

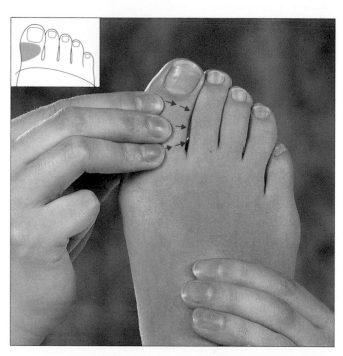

**8** To treat the vocal cords, raise your working hand over the foot *(right)*, and place the index finger on the front of the foot between the big toe and the second toe. This is where you will find the **reflex to the vocal cords**. Place the thumb of your working hand on the sole of the foot, behind your index finger, for support. Using your finger, gently rotate over this area. This reflex is important for preventive treatment, as the larynx can become inflamed – through excessive smoking or simply over using the voice.

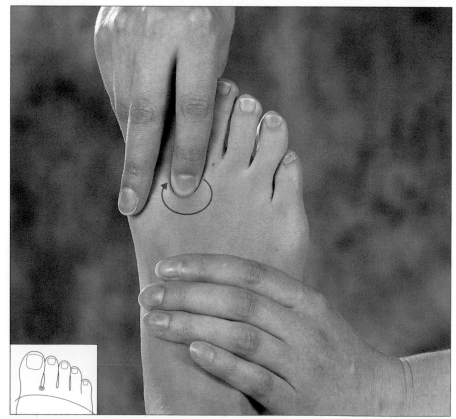

**9** The back and sides of the four smaller toes contain the **sinus reflexes** *(below)*. Support the front of the foot and gently extend the toes back. With your working fingers on the front of the toes, thumb-walk up the backs and sides of all four toes in turn, starting with the second toe.

**10** Keeping the toes extended back with your supporting hand *(below)*, move your working thumb to the medial side at the base of the second toe. This is where the **reflex area to the eyes** is located. Thumb-walk across the base of the second and third toe.

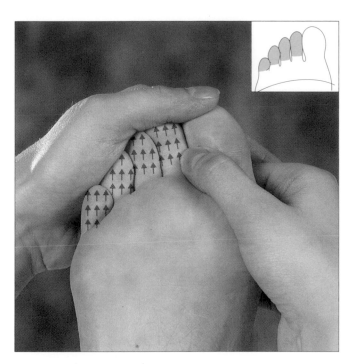

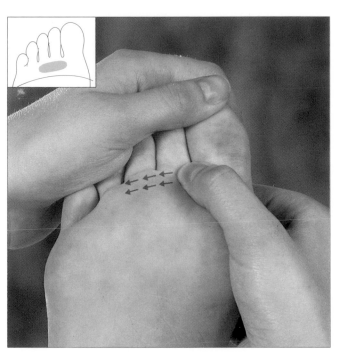

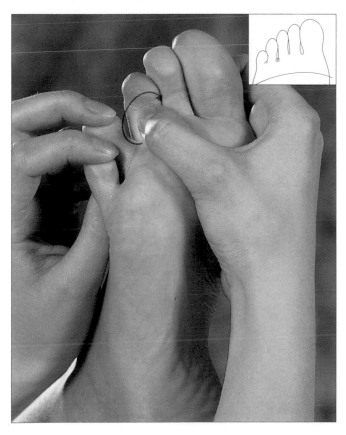

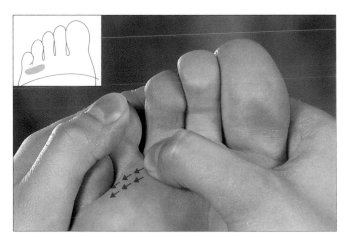

**11** Thumb-walk along the base of the toes *(left)* until you reach the web between the third and fourth toe. This is the **eustachian tube reflex** area. Gently rotate on this point with the outer edge of your thumb.

**12** To treat the **reflex area to the ears** *(above)*, thumb-walk from the eustachian tube reflex across the base of the fourth and fifth toe.

**13** The **thyroid gland reflex** is found over the top half of the ball of the big toe *(below)*. Supporting the top of the foot with your left hand, thumb-walk over this area with your working hand, using semicircular movements.

**14** Without changing the position of your hands *(below)*, work the **first parathyroid area**, at the base of the big toe. Place your working thumb on the lateral edge of the thyroid reflex and gently rotate for a few seconds.

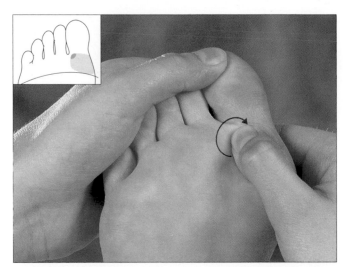

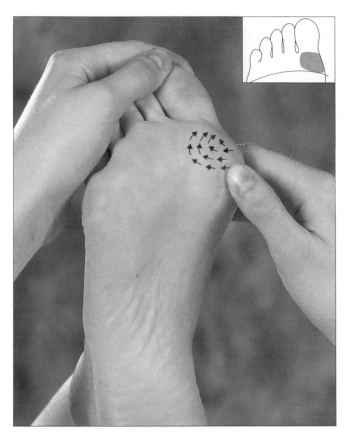

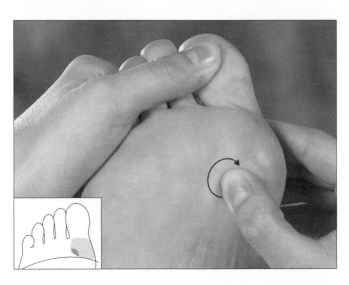

**15** Still supporting the top of the foot, move your working thumb to the base of the lateral aspect of the thyroid gland *(right)* and continue the rotary movement on the **second parathyroid area**.

**16** Now work the **teeth reflexes** on the fronts of all four toes *(right)*. Change the position of your hands by moving down the supporting left hand to the middle part of the foot. Finger-walk with the working right hand across the fronts of the second and third toes. Change hands once more to finger-walk across the fourth and fifth toes.

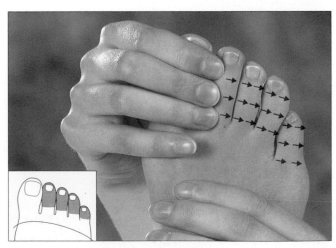

# Head and neck reflexes on the hands

Unlike the feet, the hands, due to the positioning of the thumbs, can be divided into longitudinal but not transverse zones. In order to locate the reflexes more easily, it will help to establish the waist line. This starts half-way between the little finger and the wrist and ends just below the joint of the thumb's second phalange. The head, the neck and the shoulder reflexes are situated above this line and cover the phalanges in all five longitudinal zones. The hands should be worked in the same systematic order as the feet.

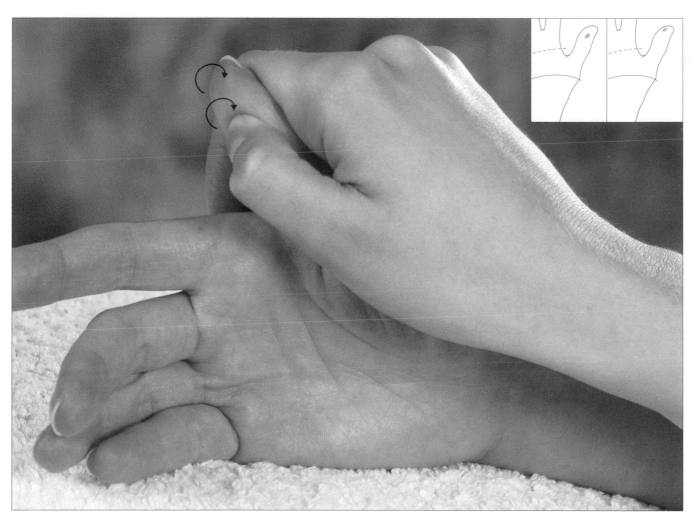

**1** Start your treatment with the **pituitary gland reflex**, which is found approximately in the centre of the fleshy pad of the thumb (above). Support the thumb with the fingers of your working hand. With the outer edge of your working thumb press and gently rotate on the pituitary reflex. This can be sensitive so if discomfort is felt, reduce the pressure while holding the back of your patient's hand with your left hand.

To treat the **reflex for the pineal gland**, keep the fingers of your working hand in the same position and simply move your working thumb to the top of the inner side of your patient's thumb. With the outer edge of your working thumb, press and gently rotate on this area. Make sure that your thumb remains constantly bent at the first joint while you are working.

**2** When you have treated the pineal gland, move your working thumb to the base of your patient's thumb on the inner edge *(right)*. This is where the **reflex to the back of the head** starts. Continue to maintain support with your left hand and, still working with the outer edge of your bent right thumb, walk in parallel lines to cover the whole length of the patient's thumb.

**3** Move to the **reflexes for the side of the neck and head** and for the **top of the brain** *(right)*. These are found along the inner border and across the top of the thumb. With your left hand, tilt the patient's palm towards you. Support the thumb with the fingers of your working hand. Thumb-walk from the base of the inner side of the patient's thumb, up the thumb's side and across the top.

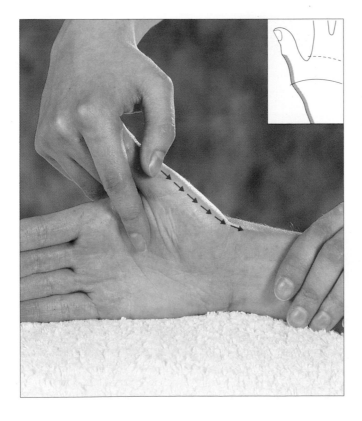

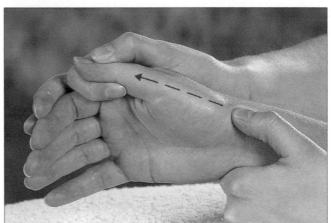

**4** Now treat the **spinal reflex**. Move your patient's hand with your supporting hand so that the back faces you *(left)*. Continue to thumb-walk down the medial border of the thumb to where the scaphoid bone joins the radius. Change over hands *(above)* and, with the thumb of your left hand, slide back up the reflex.

**5** Support the back of your patient's hand with your left hand *(below)*. Starting on the medial side of the base of your patient's thumb, where the **neck reflex** starts, take small, even steps and thumb-walk all round the base of the thumb.

**6** Change over hands. Move to the **face reflex** located on the back of the thumb *(below)*. Supporting your patient's hand with your right hand, thumb-walk in parallel lines over the back of the thumb, until all the area has been covered.

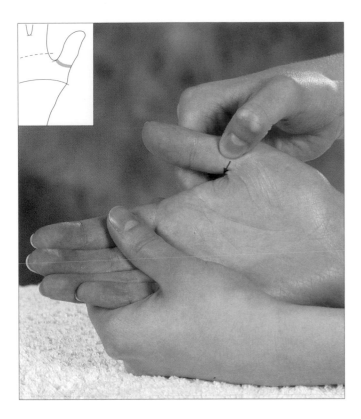

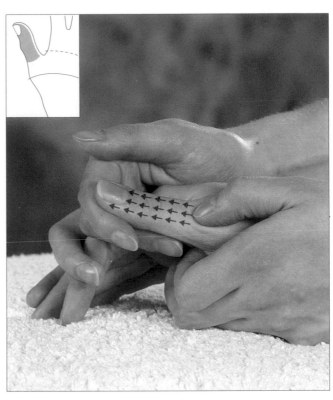

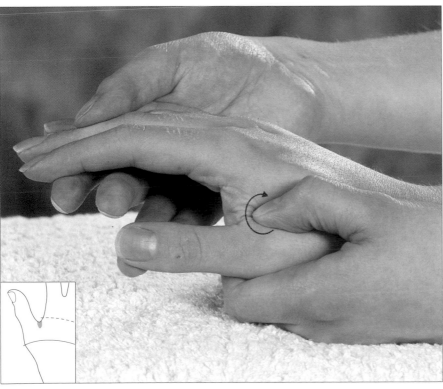

**7** Continuing to use your right hand for support, place the thumb of your working hand on the web between your patient's thumb and index finger *(left)*. This is the position for the **reflex to the vocal cords**. Supporting your patient's thumb with the fingers of your working hand, gently rotate on this point for a few seconds. This is a valuable reflex for those suffering from throat problems. If your patient is sensitive in that area, the reflex may be painful or feel gritty. In this case use a lighter pressure, or try to work with this reflex until the gritty feeling dissolves.

**8** Having treated the vocal cords, turn your patient's hand so that the back is now supported by your right hand *(below)*. Thumb-walk in parallel lines over the **sinus reflexes**. These are found on the front and sides of all four fingers.

**9** Change the position of your hands *(below)*. Starting at the base of the index finger along the medial edge, thumb-walk with your right hand across the base of this finger and the middle finger in order to treat the **eye reflex** area.

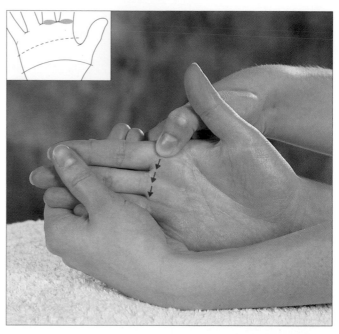

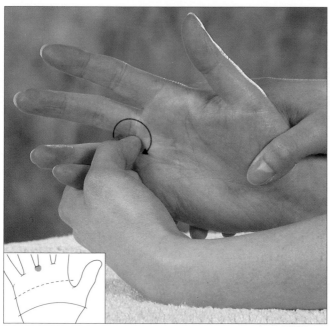

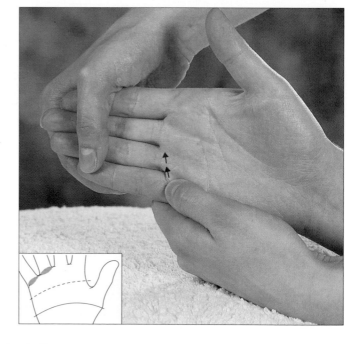

**10** Change over hands. To find the **reflex for the eustachian tube** *(above)*, separate your patient's middle and ring fingers with your supporting hand. Place the outer edge of your working thumb on the web between these fingers and rotate on this point.

**11** To work the **ear reflex**, extend your patient's fingers slightly back with your supporting hand *(above)*, and thumb-walk from the base of your patient's little finger on the lateral border to the base of the middle finger.

**12** The **thyroid gland reflex** lies over the proximal phalanx of the thumb. Use your right hand to extend the thumb back *(below)*. With the fingers of your left hand under your patient's hand, thumb-walk across this reflex, starting at the medial edge.

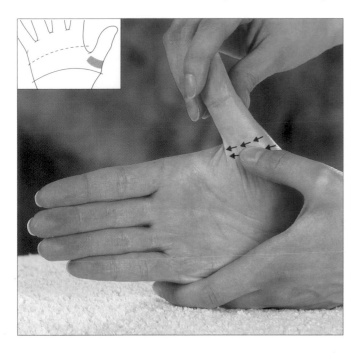

**13** Still supporting the thumb with your right hand *(below)*, slowly rotate on the **parathyroid reflexes** with your left thumb. The upper parathyroid lies in the inner upper part of the thyroid reflex; the lower parathyroid is found in the lower inner part.

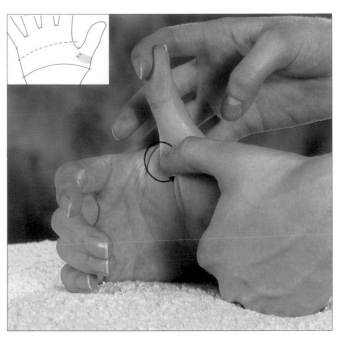

**14** Resting your patient's hand palm down on the stool *(left)*, support it by placing your right hand underneath the fingers. Using your working hand, treat the **teeth reflexes** by thumb-walking in parallel lines over the back of all four fingers. Start with the index finger and proceed to the little finger. The reflexes to the incisors cover the backs of the thumb and index finger, but you will have treated the thumb when working the reflex to the face. The reflex area for the canines is found on the back of the index finger; the reflex area for the premolars is on the back of the middle finger; the reflex area for the first and second molars is situated on the back of the ring finger; and the reflex area for the third molars, or wisdom teeth, is found on the back of the little finger.

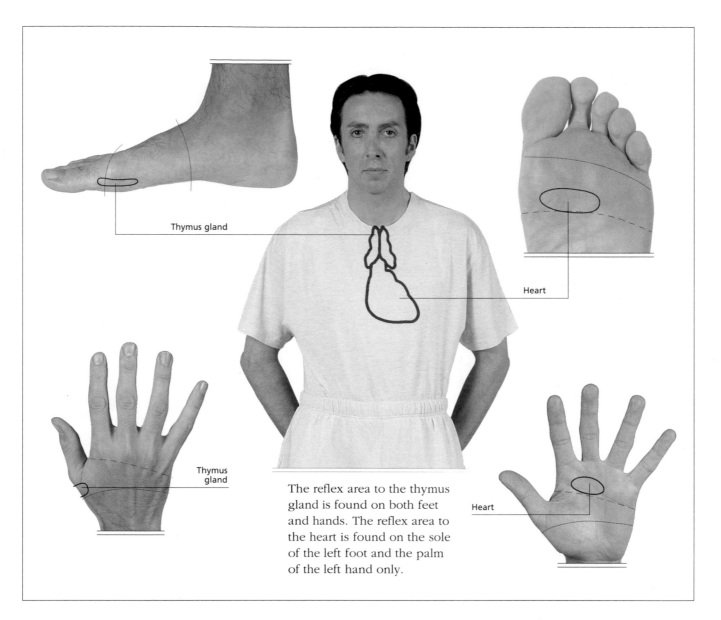

The reflex area to the thymus gland is found on both feet and hands. The reflex area to the heart is found on the sole of the left foot and the palm of the left hand only.

## Thymus gland

The thymus gland is situated in the thoracic cavity, posterior to the sternum and in front of the heart, between the lungs. It consists largely of lymphoid tissue and plays a part in the formation of lymphocytes – a type of white blood cell.

At birth this gland is relatively large and continues to increase in size until puberty, helping to develop the immune system. After puberty it gradually becomes smaller. The lymphocytes produced in infancy are coded to recognize and protect the body's tissues.

The thymus reflex is important when the immune system is not functioning correctly, especially in children who have not yet reached puberty.

## Heart

The heart is a cone-shaped organ made almost entirely of muscle, and is the centre of the circulatory system. It lies roughly in the centre of the chest, two-thirds of it to the left of the breastbone and the other third to the right. Basically, the heart consists of two pumps side by side. Blood is pumped from the right side of the heart to the lungs, where waste gases are removed and oxygen added. Freshly oxygenated blood returns to the left side of the heart from which it is pumped to all organs and tissues. This requires considerable effort, which is why the left side of the heart is bigger and more powerful than the right. The heart reflex is important for all heart and circulatory problems.

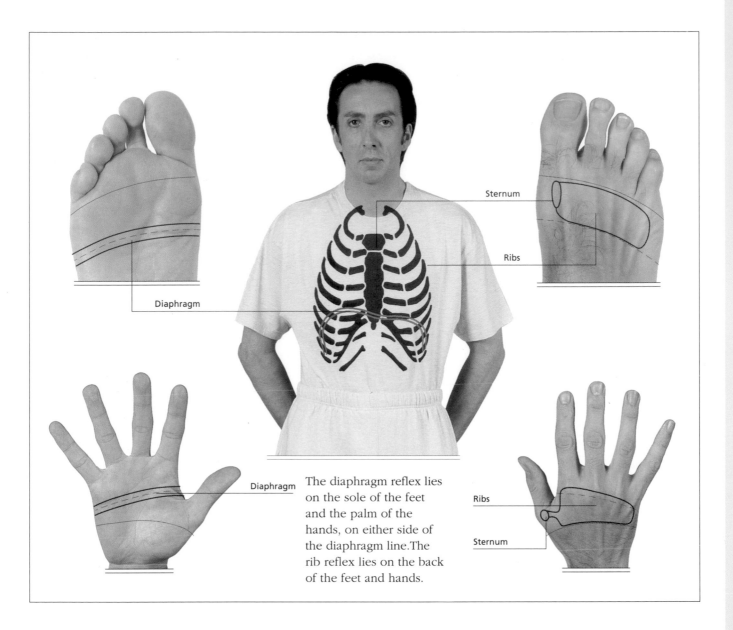

Sternum

Ribs

Diaphragm

Diaphragm

Ribs

Sternum

Diaphragm

The diaphragm reflex lies on the sole of the feet and the palm of the hands, on either side of the diaphragm line. The rib reflex lies on the back of the feet and hands.

### Ribs

Twelve pairs of ribs make up the sides of the thoracic cavity. The upper seven pairs are joined to the sternum by a strip of cartilage and are known as true ribs. The next three pairs do not join the sternum directly and are called false ribs. The eleventh and twelfth pairs are not attached to the sternum and are known as floating ribs. All the ribs are attached to and articulate with the spine.

### Sternum

The sternum, or breastbone, is a flat, narrow bone measuring about 15 centimetres (6 in) in length. It is situated in the median line of the anterior thoracic wall. To the sternum are attached the ribs and the muscles. Both the ribs and the sternum reflexes are important where damage has occured in these areas.

### Diaphragm

The diaphragm is a large, dome-shaped partition separating the cavity of the thorax from that of the abdomen, and is involved in respiration. It consists partly of muscle and partly of membrane and is attached to the circumference of the thoracic cavity; in front of the lower end of the sternum; on either side, to the lower six ribs; and at the back, to the first two lumbar vertebrae. It is drawn downwards until it is flat during inhalation. During exhalation, the diaphragm and chest muscles relax. This reflex is important in cases of hiatus hernia, and for respiratory problems.

# Shoulder and chest reflexes on the feet

Now that you have completed the reflexes to the head and neck, continue by working the reflexes for the shoulder and chest. These reflexes are all found above the diaphragm. To locate the diaphragm, visualize a line starting at the lower end of the ball of the big toe and extending across the sole of the foot. When you treat the lung area you may find that this feels gritty. One reason could be the level of pollution present in the air, or excessive smoking on the part of your patient. With regular treatment, this can be cleared.

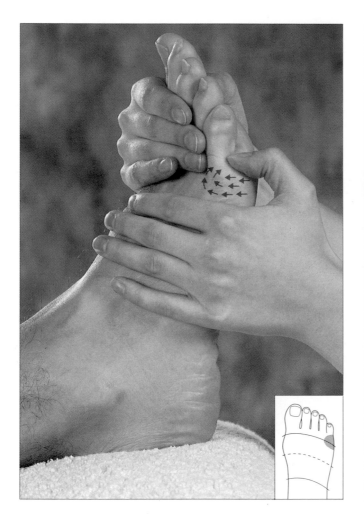

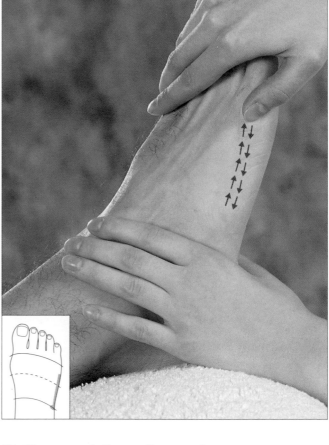

**1** Start this part of your treatment with the **shoulder reflex** *(above)*. This is located in the base and lateral side of the little toe. Supporting the foot with your right hand, place the thumb of your working hand at the lateral edge of the base of the little toe. Thumb-walk several times in semicircles over this reflex, making sure that you cover the whole area. If your patient is experiencing pain, work a little longer over the reflex.

**2** The **arm and elbow reflex** extends from the shoulder reflex along the lateral edge of the fifth metatarsal bone on the side and top of the foot *(above)*. Change over hands, so that your supporting hand rests just above the ankle joint. Place the fingers of your right hand over the top of the foot. Starting at the lateral edge, thumb-walk down the reflex; then change hands to thumb-walk with your left hand back up the reflex.

**3** Supporting the foot and toes with your left hand *(below)*, work the **trachea reflex**. Thumb-walk from the medial side of the big toe base, along the medial edge of the ball.

**4** The **reflex area for the right lung** is found in all five zones of the right foot *(below)*. The left lung reflex is on the left foot. Thumb-walk in horizontal lines across this reflex.

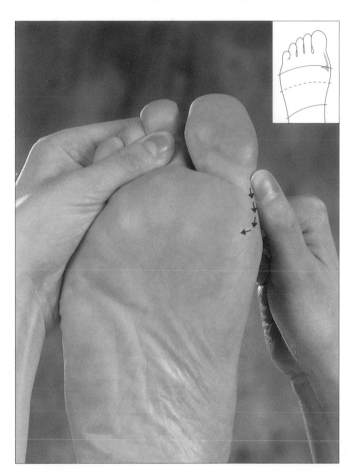

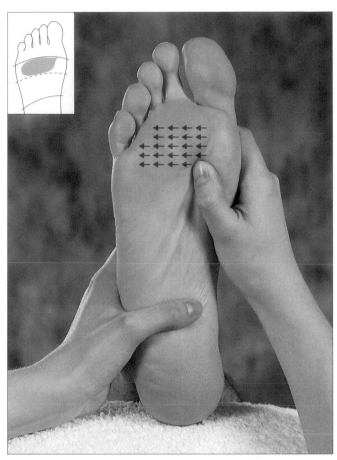

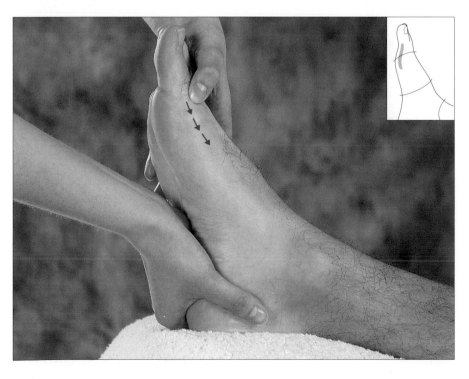

**5** To treat the **thymus gland**, change hands and wrap your supporting hand around the heel of the foot, with the thumb on the medial side *(left)*. With your left hand gently flex the foot towards you. Place the outer edge of your left thumb onto the front of the foot in zone one. Starting from the medial side at the base of the big toe, thumb-walk down the front of the foot from this point to the end of the third phalanges. This reflex is part of the immune system, playing its biggest role before puberty.

**6** The **heart reflex** area is found on the left foot only *(below)*. Support the foot with your right hand. Thumb-walk from the metatarsal bone, covering zones two and three.

**7** Move your working fingers to the **rib reflex** on the top of the foot, a supporting thumb on the sole *(below)*. From the fifth metatarsal bone, finger-walk across the foot.

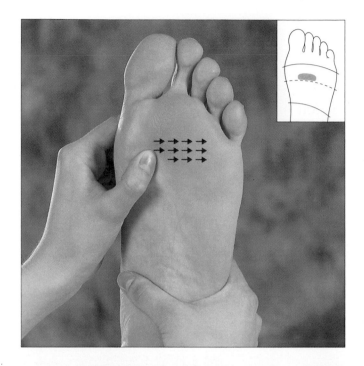

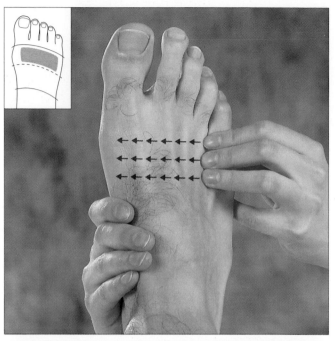

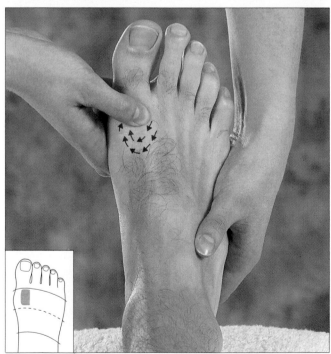

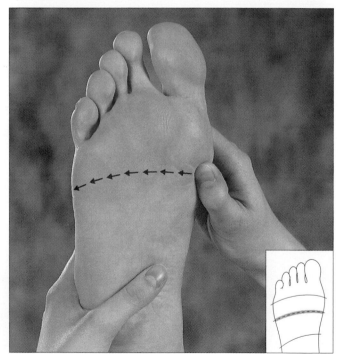

**8** Support the foot with your left hand *(above)*, and place your right thumb below the base on the front of the big toe, in zone one. Gently thumb-walk around this area to treat the **sternum reflex**.

**9** To complete this section of the foot, use your right thumb to walk across the **diaphragm reflex** *(above)*. This area lies either side of a line drawn across the foot, starting beneath the ball of the big toe.

# Shoulder and chest reflexes on the hands

On the hands, the reflexes for the shoulders and chest are found in the area between the base of the fingers and a line running a quarter of the way down across the palm of the hand. This line represents the diaphragm. Due to the position of the thumb, which can vary in individuals, the diaphragm is not normally shown; but because the area afforded to some hand reflexes is much smaller than on the feet, greater precision is required when locating them. When you treat the reflex to the heart, remember that it is only found on the left foot or hand, and care should be taken with people suffering from heart disease.

**1** Start by working the **shoulder reflex** *(above)*. This extends around the base of the little finger, on the lateral side of the finger and on the back of the hand. Support the back of the hand with your right hand.

Place the fingers of your working hand beneath your patient's hand for extra support. Then, using the outer edge of your working thumb, walk several times around the base of the little finger.

63

**2** When you have completed work on the **shoulder reflex**, change over hands *(right)* and using your left hand to support the patient's hand, tilt it towards you. Place the outer edge of your right thumb onto the lateral side of the shoulder reflex where the **reflex to the arm and elbow** begins Thumb-walk until you reach the waist line. Change the position of your hands again *(below right)*, and with the outer edge of your left thumb, slide back up the reflex.

**3** Change over hands once more *(below)* so that you can support the back of your patient's hand with your left hand, and the fingers with your working hand. Place your working thumb on the lateral side at the base of the index finger. This is where you will find the beginning of the **lung reflex**. Thumb-walk across zones two to five, in the area between the base of the fingers and the diaphragm line.

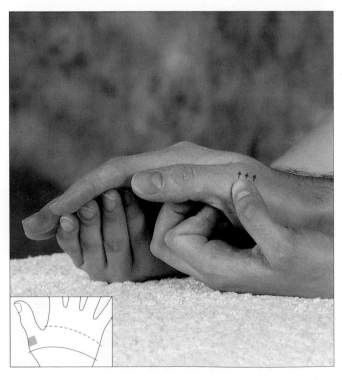

**4** To treat the **thymus gland** located over the medial half of the ball of the thumb *(right)*, turn over your patient's hand. Support the palm of the hand with your right hand and thumb-walk across this reflex.

**5** From the thymus gland, work the **reflex to the heart**. This is positioned on the palm of the left hand *(left)*, in zones two and three, just above the diaphragm line. Supporting the back of your patient's hand with your right hand, thumb-walk across this area with your working hand. Remember that this reflex is found only on the left hand.

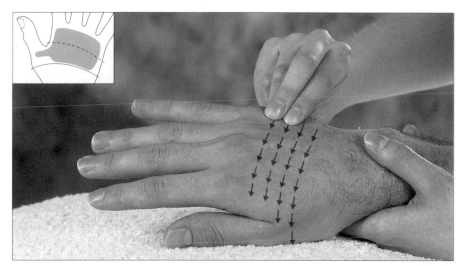

**6** Now work the **rib reflex** *(left)*. This is found in all five zones on the back of the hand, and covers the area from the base of the fingers to the diaphragm. Supporting the patient's hand with your left hand, walk across this reflex with the index and middle fingers of your right hand.

**7** Finally, treat the **reflex to the sternum** *(below)*. This is in zone one, on the medial edge of the head of the metacarpal. With your supporting hand in the same position, gently rotate on this point with the thumb of your right hand.

# Abdomen reflexes

The reflexes to the abdomen are found beneath the diaphragm in the second and third transverse zones. These zones cover the lower half of the metatarsals to the upper part of the calcaneum on the feet, and the lower half of the metacarpals to the wrists on the hands. They include all the organs which constitute the digestive system. Their functions are described below. Other organs found in the abdomen have been included under lower body reflexes *(see page 84)* since they are located mainly on the medial and lateral borders of the feet and hands. These reflexes would therefore be treated only after completing treatment on the soles of the feet or the palms of the hands.

### Solar plexus

The anterior branches of the spinal nerves (except for two of them) do not go directly to the structures of the body they supply. Instead, they form networks on either side of the body by joining with adjacent nerves. Such a network is called a plexus. The solar plexus – resembling sun rays – is situated behind the stomach. It is an important reflex wherever tension or stress are present.

### Liver

The liver is the largest solid organ of the body. It is situated in the upper part of the abdomen, beneath the diaphragm and mainly on the right side of the body. It is divided into a large right lobe and a smaller tapering left lobe. The liver undertakes many chemical activities. It neutralizes toxic substances from the small intestine, produces bile which assists digestion, and stores vitamins and glycogen; it manufactures enzymes, cholesterol, complex proteins, vitamin A and blood coagulation factors; it is also involved in carbohydrate, fat and protein metabolism. This is an important reflex where the body is overly toxic, and for diseases such as hepatitis and jaundice.

### Gall bladder

The gall bladder is a sac of approximately 7.5 centimetres (3 in) in length, found on the under-surface of the right lobe of the liver. Its function is to store and concentrate the bile, secreted by the liver, that helps break down fatty foods. In order to participate in the digestive process, bile is ejected, by muscle contraction, through the bile duct and into the small intestine. This is an important reflex for gall stones and in conditions where the digestion of fat is difficult.

### Spleen

The spleen is a very large lymph gland lying on the upper left side of the abdomen. In addition to producing lymphocytes – a type of white blood cell – the spleen also removes old and malformed red cells from the bloodstream and breaks them down. This is an important reflex when building up defence against infection.

### Oesophagus

The oesophagus is a muscular tube that runs from the back of the throat, through the neck and chest, to the stomach. After swallowing, food passes along this tube to the stomach by rhythmic contractions of the oesophageal muscles. Situated at the base of the oesophagus is a muscular valve which relaxes and opens to allow food into the stomach, but also prevents the acid contents of the stomach from flowing back into the oesophagus where they can cause irritation. This is an important reflex where there is difficulty in swallowing.

### Stomach

The stomach is located behind the lower ribs, mainly to the left side of the body, and is shaped like a J. The lower end represents the pylorus; the top end of the J is where the oesophagus reaches the stomach. When food enters the stomach, powerful muscles in the

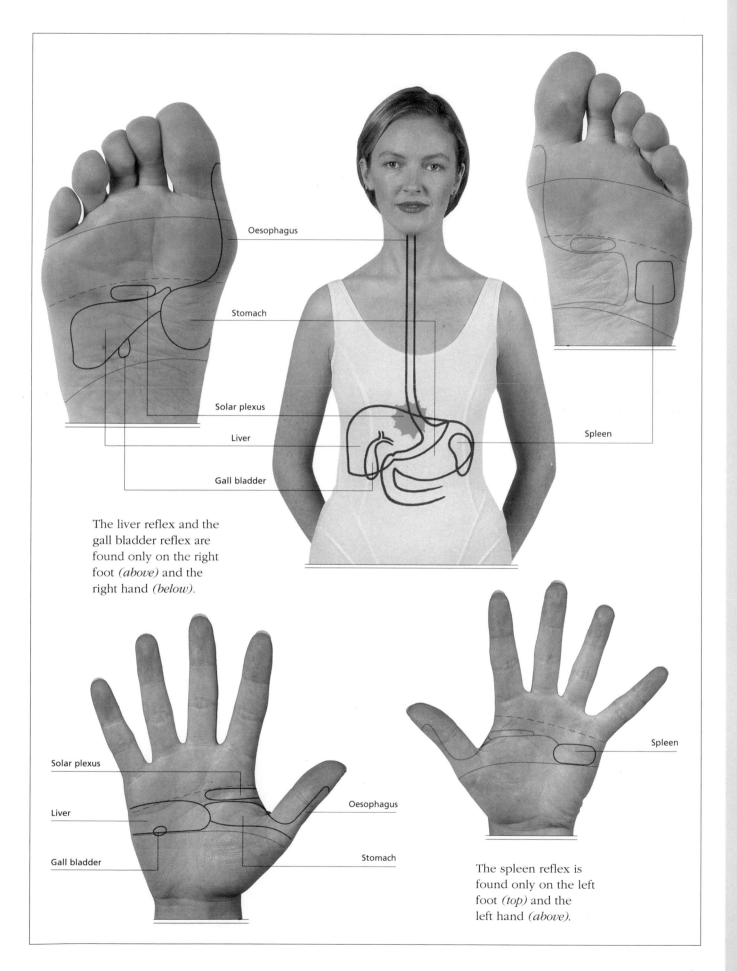

Oesophagus

Stomach

Solar plexus

Liver

Gall bladder

Spleen

The liver reflex and the gall bladder reflex are found only on the right foot *(above)* and the right hand *(below)*.

Solar plexus

Liver

Gall bladder

Oesophagus

Stomach

Spleen

The spleen reflex is found only on the left foot *(top)* and the left hand *(above)*.

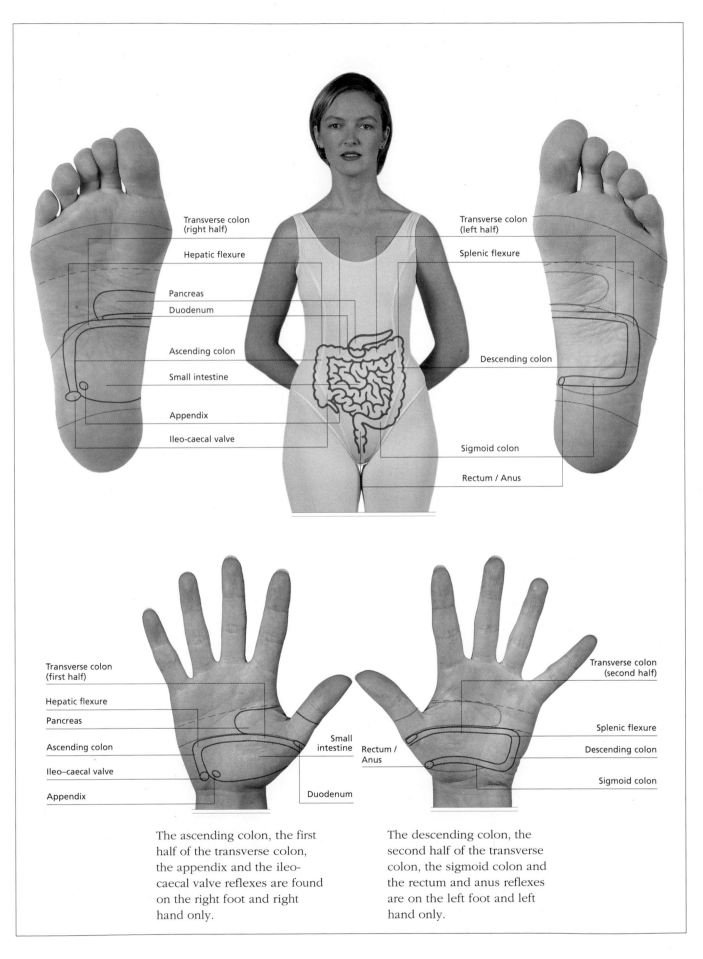

Transverse colon
(right half)

Transverse colon
(left half)

Hepatic flexure

Splenic flexure

Pancreas

Duodenum

Ascending colon

Descending colon

Small intestine

Appendix

Ileo-caecal valve

Sigmoid colon

Rectum / Anus

Transverse colon
(first half)

Transverse colon
(second half)

Hepatic flexure

Pancreas

Splenic flexure

Ascending colon

Small
intestine

Rectum /
Anus

Descending colon

Ileo–caecal valve

Sigmoid colon

Appendix

Duodenum

The ascending colon, the first
half of the transverse colon,
the appendix and the ileo-
caecal valve reflexes are found
on the right foot and right
hand only.

The descending colon, the
second half of the transverse
colon, the sigmoid colon and
the rectum and anus reflexes
are on the left foot and left
hand only.

stomach wall start to crush and mix it with the hydrochloric acid and digestive enzymes manufactured there. The main digestive enzyme is pepsin, which breaks down protein foods such as meat. This enzyme is only active when there is acid present. The semi-digested food then passes through the pyloric sphincter into the duodenum. This reflex is important for problems relating to the stomach such as ulcers, cancer, indigestion and heartburn and for general digestive problems.

## Pancreas

The pancreas lies behind the stomach. Part of the endocrine system, it is a double-purpose gland with many branched ducts. Its small clusters of islet cells secrete insulin, a hormone which is essential for utilizing sugars, and without which diabetes may develop. Many of the foods we eat contain glucose, the main source of energy for all the cells in our body. Insulin stimulates those cells to absorb enough glucose from the blood for the energy they need. It then activates the liver to absorb and store the surplus. The mass of pancreatic cells produce pancreatic juices which pass along the pancreatic duct into the duodenum where they help break down carbohydrates, proteins and fats. The pancreas reflex is important for certain digestive disorders, for hyper- and hypoglycaemia, and for diabetes.

## Small intestine

The small intestine is a tube about 5 to 6 metres (about 17 ft) long and is divided into the duodenum, the jejunum and the ileum. It is the main site for the absorption of nutrients into the bloodstream. The semi-digested food from the stomach passes into the duodenum, where the digestive process is furthered by the secretion of enzymes, bile from the gall bladder and pancreatic juice from the pancreas. Food is pushed along the small intestine by peristaltic waves of contractions of the muscles in its walls. Once the food molecules are small enough, they pass through the thin lining of the intestine into the bloodstream and then on to the liver for storage and distribution. The small intestine reflex is important

for all diseases affecting the digestive tract. Disorders of this type include Crohn's disease, coeliac disease and digestive problems.

## Appendix

The appendix is a thin worm-shaped pouch, about 7.5 centimetres (3 in) long, that projects from the first part of the large intestine. In herbivorous animals the appendix is relatively large compared with humans, and plays an important role in the digestive process. In human beings the appendix is considered to be an evolutionary relic. It is an important reflex where there is suspected appendicitis.

## Ileo-caecal valve

The ileo-caecal valve is a fold of mucous membrane which guards the opening from the ileum to the large intestine. It allows materials from the small intestine to pass into the large intestine and prevents a backflow from the large to small intestine. This is an important reflex in cases of constipation.

## Large intestine (colon)

The large intestine is about 1.5 metres (5 feet) long and consists of two main organs: the colon and the rectum. The colon is divided into several sections. The ascending colon ascends on the right side of the abdomen to the undersurface of the liver. Here it bends to the left (hepatic flexure) and continues as the transverse colon, across the abdomen to the lower end of the spleen. At this point it curves (splenic flexure) and passes down the left side of the body as the descending colon. The last section is the sigmoid colon. It projects inwards to the midline and terminates as the rectum. The rectum is a short tube of about 12.5 centimetres (5 in) in length leading to the anus. Fluid and various mineral salts from the intestinal contents are absorbed into the bloodstream through the membranous wall of the colon. The semisolid faeces that remain move down into the rectum, from where they are eventually excreted as stools. This reflex is important in cases of constipation, irritable bowel syndrome, diverticulosis, ulcerative colitis and diarrhoea.

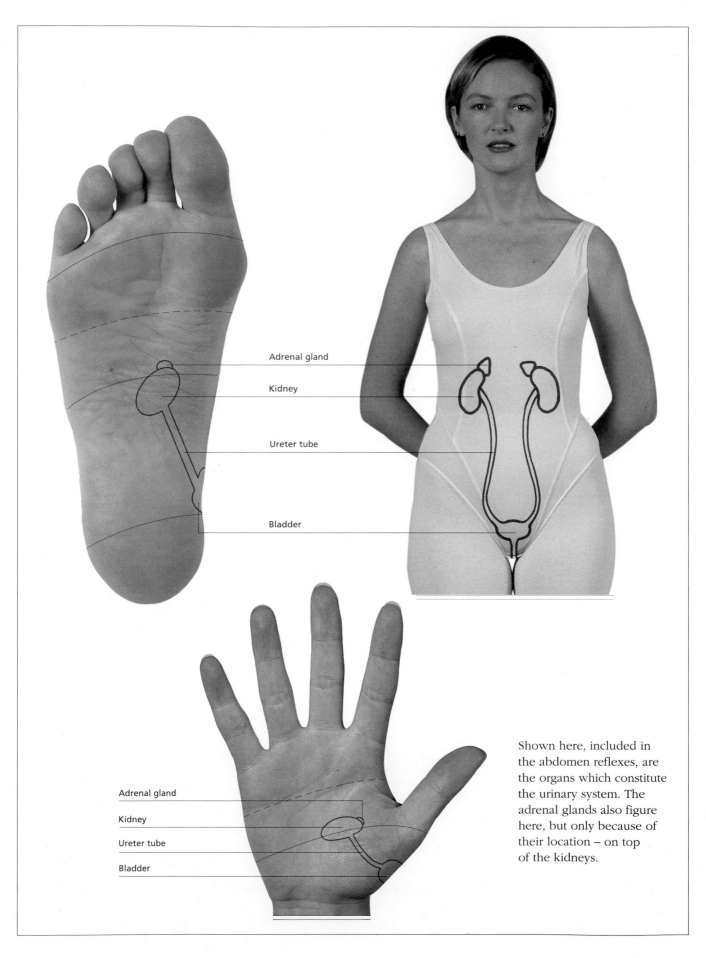

Adrenal gland

Kidney

Ureter tube

Bladder

Adrenal gland

Kidney

Ureter tube

Bladder

Shown here, included in the abdomen reflexes, are the organs which constitute the urinary system. The adrenal glands also figure here, but only because of their location – on top of the kidneys.

## Bladder

The urinary bladder is a hollow muscular organ situated in the pelvic cavity. Its function is to store urine which trickles down the ureter tubes from the kidneys. In a male the bladder is directly anterior to the rectum. In a female it is anterior to the vagina and inferior to the uterus. The bladder has elastic flexible walls which allow it to expand as it fills and then contract through the relaxed sphincter muscle when urinating. When the bladder contracts, urine is prevented from flowing back up the ureter tubes by valves that link the ureters to the bladder. The urine is expelled from the bladder through the urethra. The male urethra, which is longer than the female, also provides an outlet for semen. The bladder reflex is important for all conditions related to the urinary tract, for example cystitis.

## Ureter tubes

The body has two ureter tubes which are approximately 25 to 30 centimetres (about 12 in) long. The purpose of the ureters is to carry urine from the kidneys to the bladder. The reflexes to the ureter tubes are important when kidney stones are present, and for all infections to the urinary system.

## Kidneys

The kidneys are bean-shaped, deep maroon in colour and weigh about 150 grams (5 oz) They are approximately 10 centimetres (4 in) long and 5 centimetres (2 in) wide, and are situated above the waist on either side of the spinal column, below the lowest ribs. The right kidney, which lies just below the liver, is usually lower than the left. Both kidneys are surrounded by fat which cushions and supports them. The kidneys receive their blood supply from the renal artery. This artery divides into progressively smaller branches which infiltrate the kidney tissue and filtering units. The blood is collected by an intricate system of small veins, which join to form larger vessels that empty into the renal vein, returning blood to the general circulation. Kidney cells also manufacture substances which help to control blood pressure. When the blood supply to the kidneys is diminished, these substances are manufactured in larger amounts, and cause raised blood pressure in an attempt to increase the blood flow through the kidneys. Each kidney contains over one million tiny filtering units, called glomeruli, which remove waste chemicals and excess water from the blood travelling through them. The filtered liquid passes from the glomeruli to the central section of the kidney along a long thin tubule, which is surrounded by blood vessels. These blood vessels reabsorb the nutrients from the liquid. The remaining urine continues along the tubule into the ureter and into the bladder. This is a very important reflex for infections and for all problems relating to the urinary system.

## Adrenal glands

The adrenal glands are two small triangular bodies lying just above the kidneys. They consist of the medulla, which forms the inner portion of the gland, and the cortex which forms the outer part which is composed of layered glandular cells. The medulla secretes adrenaline and noradrenaline which is vital in energizing the body to meet sudden dangers and alarms and which also plays an important part in controlling heart rate and blood pressure. The cortex secretes steroid hormones which are closely linked in structure but differing in activity. The adrenal reflexes are important in cases of hormonal imbalance, stress, arthritis, asthma and allergies.

# Abdomen reflexes on the feet

The reflexes for the abdomen cover an area on either side of the waist line on the sole of the foot. Look at the chart of reflexes to familiarize yourself with the position of the abdominal organs. Then work the reflexes step by step, following the order of treatment given below. Make sure that you treat both feet. First complete the treatment on the right foot, and then on the left foot. Remember that some reflexes are found on one foot only. For example, the liver reflex is found on the right foot only, the spleen reflex on the left foot only, and so on. Whenever you find some spots to be tender, reduce the pressure.

**1** Holding and supporting the toes with your left hand *(right)*, press the **solar plexus reflex** with the thumb of your working hand. It lies just below the diaphragm line, between the second and third zones. Gently rotate on this point in a clockwise direction.

**2** The **liver reflex** is found only on the right foot *(below)* and looks similar to an unequal-sided triangle. Its longest side sits just below the diaphragm and covers all five zones. Its shortest side lies between the diaphragm and the waist line. Holding the foot with your right hand, bend the toes back slightly to open up the reflex areas. With the outer edge of your left thumb, walk horizontally across the reflex, following the shape of the triangle.

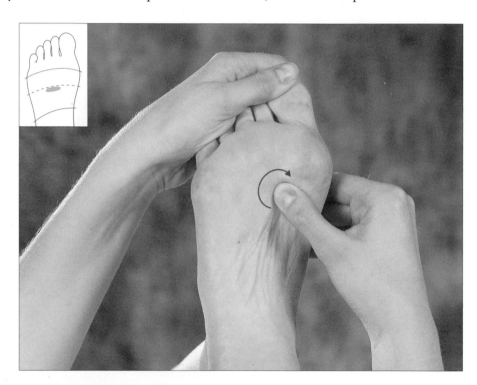

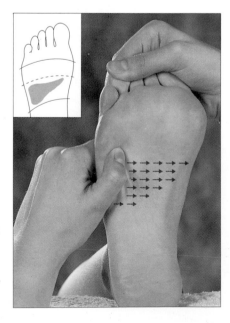

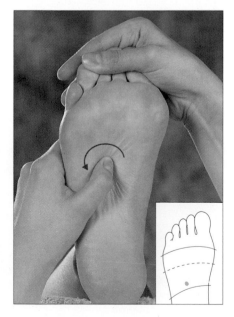

**3** Without moving your supporting hand *(left)*, locate the **gall bladder reflex**. This is found on the right foot only and lies in zone three, just below the liver reflex, and approximately one finger's width above the waist line. Although this is an important reflex, it is also very small and sometimes difficult to find, so you will find the chart of reflexes helpful. Then, with your working thumb, rotate in an anticlockwise direction.

**4** The **splenic reflex** is found only on the left foot. It lies in zones four and five, below the diaphragm and just above the waist line *(right)*. Change the position of your hands so that your right hand becomes the working one. Holding the foot with your left hand, bend the toes back slightly. Thumb-walk with your working hand across this area in horizontal lines.

**5** Prior to treating the stomach reflex, the **reflex for the oesophagus** is worked *(below)*. This is found on the medial side of the foot in zone one, leading down from the big toe to just below the diaphragm. Supporting the heel of the foot with your right hand, thumb-walk down this reflex.

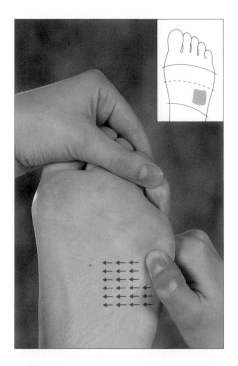

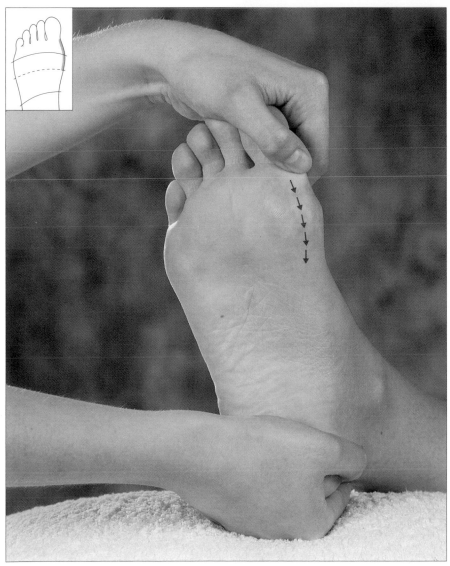

**6** From the oesophagus, continue the treatment by working on the **reflex to the stomach** *(below)*. This is found in both feet, between the diaphragm and the waist line. On the right foot, the reflex area covers zone one. On the left foot it covers zones one, two and three. Bending back the toes with your supporting hand, thumb-walk horizontally across this area with your working hand.

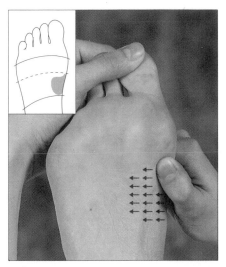

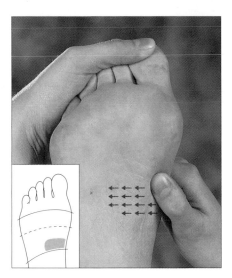

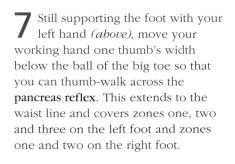

**7** Still supporting the foot with your left hand *(above)*, move your working hand one thumb's width below the ball of the big toe so that you can thumb-walk across the **pancreas reflex**. This extends to the waist line and covers zones one, two and three on the left foot and zones one and two on the right foot.

**8** With your supporting hand, bend the toes back to help you locate the tendon on the sole of the foot *(right)*. Then move your working thumb down in zone one to the medial side of this tendon, where it crosses the waist line. This is the **duodenum reflex**. Rotate gently on this point in a clockwise direction.

**9** The **reflex area for the small intestine** *(below)* lies on the medial side of the foot, below the waist line, at the start of the tarsal bones and covers zones one to four on both feet. With your right thumb, walk across the top of this reflex. Then change hands and thumb-walk back with your left hand. Cover the whole area.

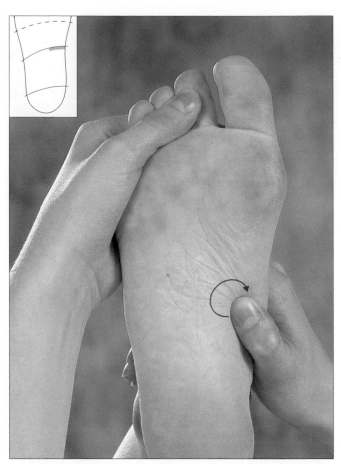

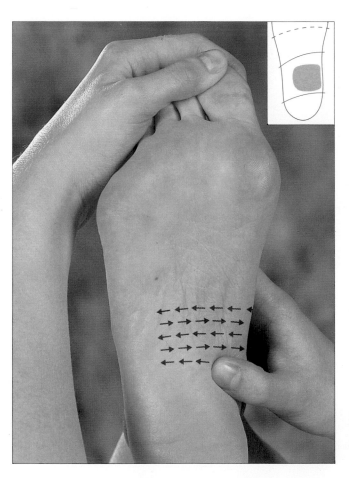

**10** Now find the **appendix reflex**. This is located *(right)* over the tarsal bones, just above the pelvic floor in zone four, on the right foot only. With the thumb of your right hand, slowly rotate on this reflex in a clockwise direction.

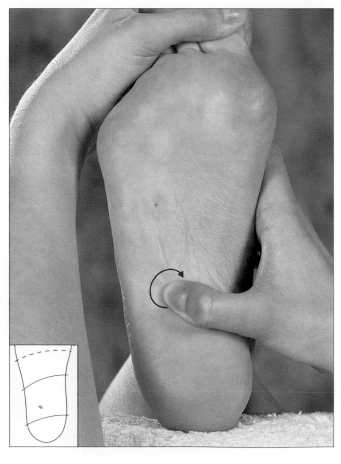

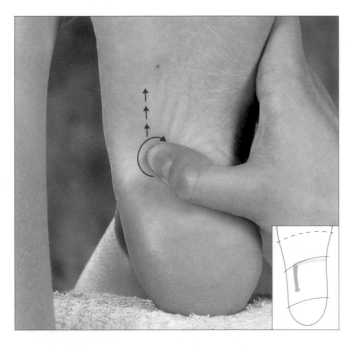

**11** Just above the appendix reflex, in zones four and five, you will find the **reflex for the ileo-caecal valve** *(left)*. Without changing the position of your hands, gently rotate on this point with your working thumb. When you have completed this, continue to thumb-walk up the foot in zones four and five to waist level to treat the **ascending colon reflex**. Note that this reflex and those for the ileo-caecal valve and appendix are found only on the right foot. When you have reached waist level, press three or four times on that point to treat the **hepatic flexure**. This is where the large intestine bends before passing across the abdomen.

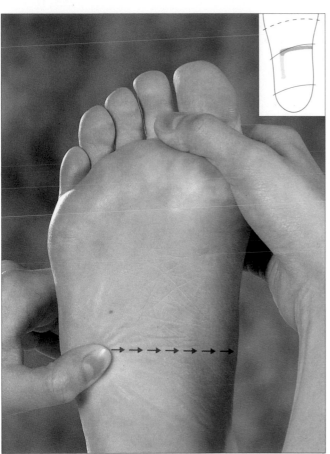

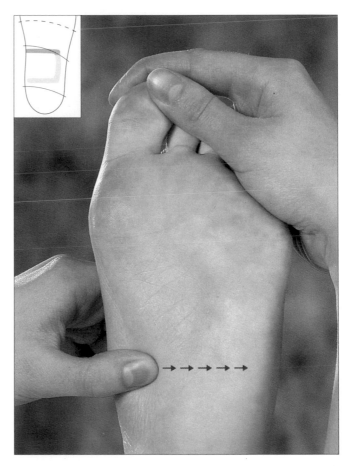

**12** Change hands, and thumb-walk at waist level *(above)* across all five zones. To treat the transverse colon, start with the first half which lies on the right side of the body. The first part of the **transverse colon reflex area** is found on the right foot.

**13** The remainder of the **transverse colon** is found on the left foot *(above)*. Treat it when you work that foot. Thumb-walk across to the medial border of zone five, where the **splenic flexure** is found. Gently press two or three times on this point.

**14** To work the **reflex area for the descending colon**, support the foot with your left hand *(below)*. Thumb-walk in zones four and five to the base of the calcaneum, and press on the **sigmoid flexure** a few times.

**15** Without changing hands *(below)*, thumb-walk across the foot to the **sigmoid colon reflex** on the medial side of zone one. If your patient suffers from constipation, this reflex may feel lumpy and tender.

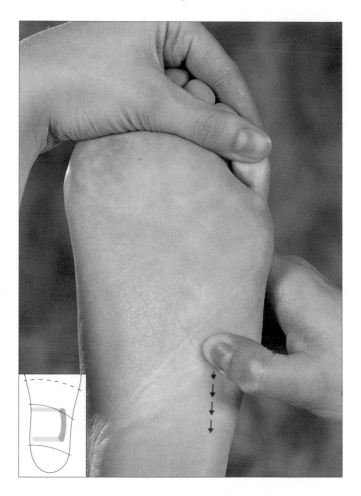

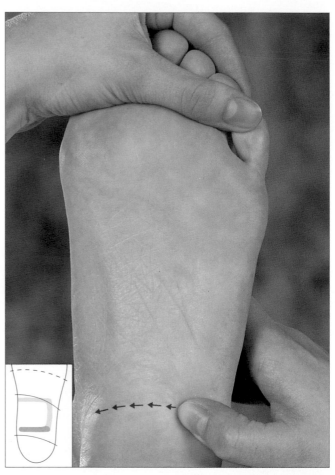

**16** When your thumb has reached the medial side of zone one *(right)*, slowly rotate on this point, in an anticlockwise direction, for a few seconds. This is the **reflex for the rectum and anus**. The rectum is linked to the anus by the anal canal. The anus is the opening at the end of the rectum through which undigested residues are voided. This reflex is found on the left foot only.

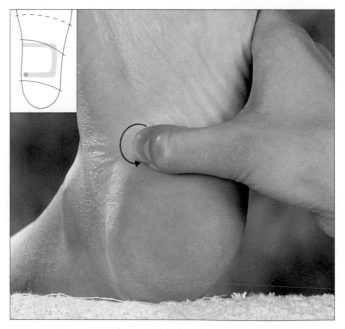

**17** Supporting the heel of the foot with your working hand *(below)*, use your working thumb to walk over the **bladder reflex**, the slightly puffy area found on the medial side of the foot.

**18** From the bladder reflex, thumb-walk up the **ureter tube reflex**, across zones two and three *(below)* to waist level. To find it easily, gently bend the toes back and follow the path of the tendon.

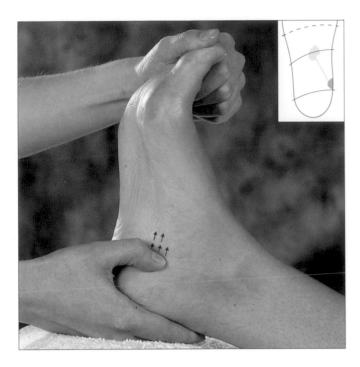

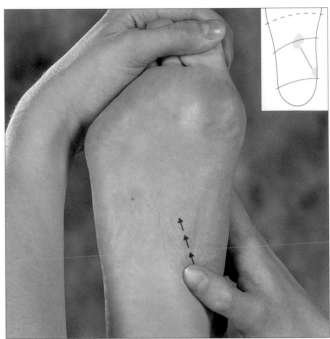

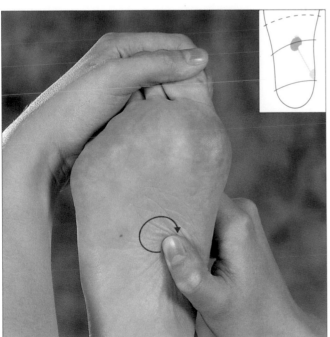

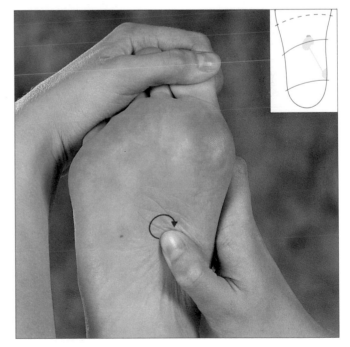

**19** You will find the **reflex to the right kidney** at the end of the ureter tube *(above)*, in zones two and three, at waist level. With your working thumb, slowly rotate on this point in a clockwise direction.

**20** Close to the kidney reflex in zone two, just above the waist level, is the **reflex to the right adrenal gland** *(above)*. Move your working thumb to this position and work this point with a rotating movement.

# Abdomen reflexes on the hands

Before starting your treatment, locate the diaphragm and waist line on the hands to help you find the reflex areas. To position the waist line, find a point midway between the base of the little finger and the wrist.

Imagine a line extending across the hand to zone two, descending and crossing the thumb. For the diaphragm, take a straight line across the palm of the hand, starting quarterway from the base of the little finger to the wrist.

1 Start your treatment with the **solar plexus reflex**. This is found at the level of the diaphragm line in zones two and three *(right)*. Use your left hand as the supporting hand. Place the fingers of your right hand at the back of your patient's hand. With the outer edge of your working thumb, press and rotate in a clockwise direction over the reflex.

2 The **liver reflex** is found only on the right hand *(below left)* or foot. It lies between the diaphragm and waist line in zones three, four and five and covers the lower half of the metacarpals. Use your left thumb to walk in horizontal lines across this reflex area. Start just below the diaphragm line in zone five.

3 Continue by rotating your working thumb *(below right)* on the **reflex of the gall bladder**, located in the palm of the hand, just above waist level in zone three. This reflex is found only on the right hand or foot.

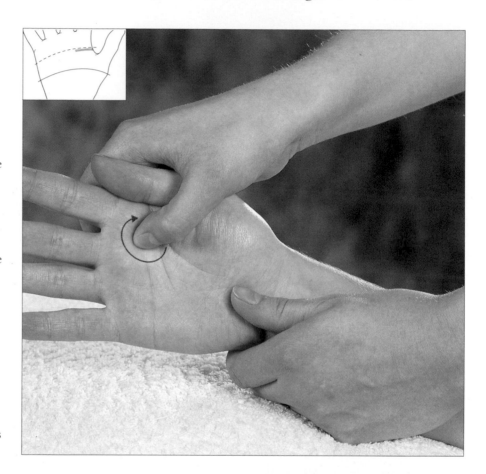

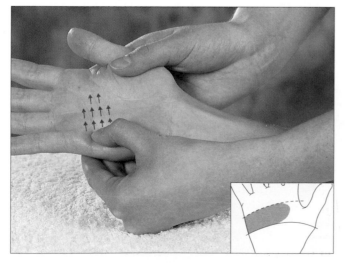

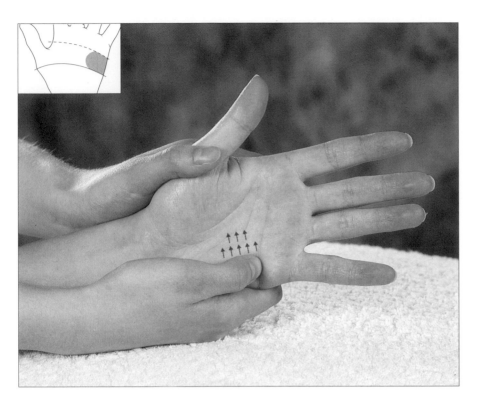

**4** Supporting the back of your patient's hand with your left hand *(left)*, use your right thumb to walk in horizontal lines across the **reflex area for the spleen**. It is positioned between the diaphragm line and the waist line in zones four and five, and is found only on the left hand, and the left foot. Begin thumb-walking at the lateral edge of zone five, just below the diaphragm line.

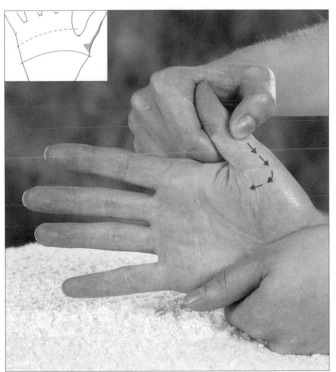

**5** The **reflex for the oesophagus** is found on the medial aspect of both thumbs *(above)*. It starts at the joint of the first and second phalanges and follows a straight line down the thumb to the head of the metacarpal bone. Using your left hand for support, thumb-walk down this reflex with your working hand.

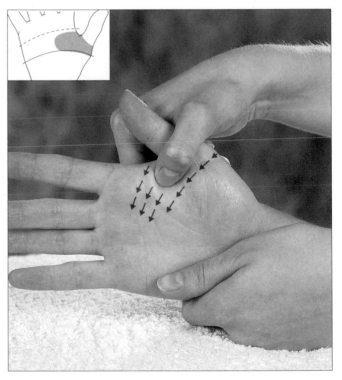

**6** Continue to thumb-walk with your working hand *(above)* over the **reflex area for the stomach**, which joins the end of the oesophagus reflex area. It is found below the diaphram and above the waist line in zone one on the palm of the right hand, but in zones one, two and three on the palm of the left hand.

**7** The **pancreas reflex** covers only zones one and two on the right hand *(right)*, but it covers zones one, two and three on the left hand. Supporting the patient's hand with your left hand, place your working thumb on the medial edge of your patient's thumb, one finger's width above the waist line. Now thumb-walk horizontally across this reflex until you reach the waist line.

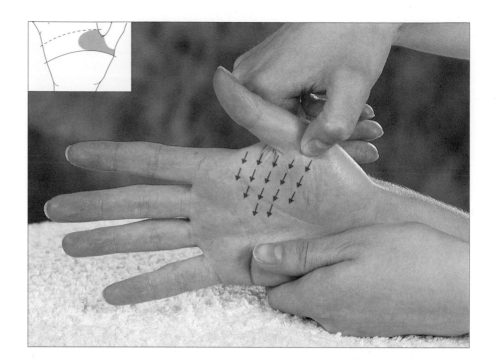

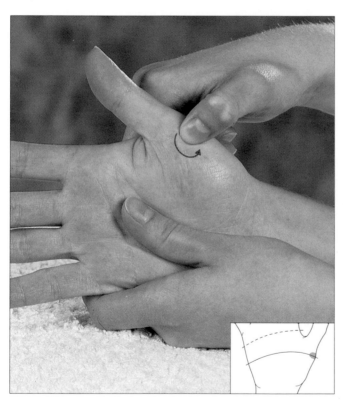

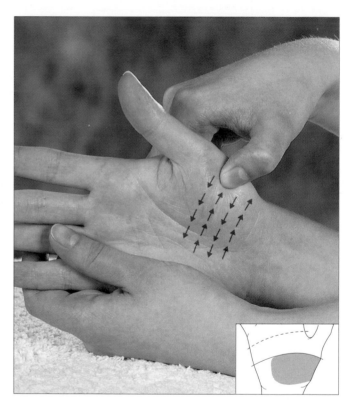

**8** The **reflex for the duodenum** is situated on the waist line in zone one, on the medial aspect of the thumb *(above)*. The duodenum forms the first part of the small intestine. Supporting your patient's hand with your left hand, gently rotate on this reflex with the outer edge of your right thumb.

**9** The **small intestine reflex** extends over zones one, two, three and four and covers the area of the metacarpal bones lying below the waist line. From the medial side of your patient's thumb *(above)*, thumb-walk across the palm to the end of zone four. Change hands and thumb-walk back to cover the area.

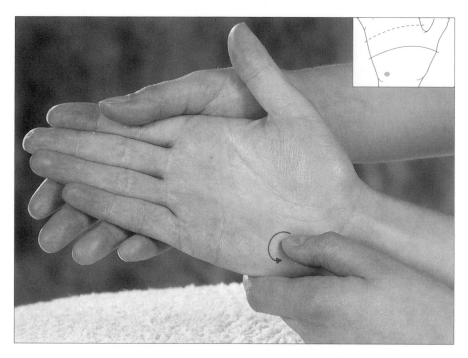

**10** The **appendix reflex** is found on the right hand and foot only *(left)*. Remember to omit this step when you treat the left hand. Supporting the patient's hand with your right hand, place your left thumb on the lateral side of zone four, over the carpal bones. Your working-hand fingers rest on the back of your patient's hand. With your working thumb, gently rotate this point.

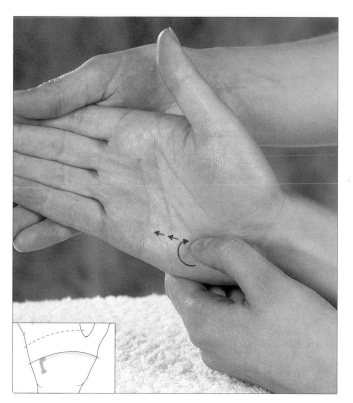

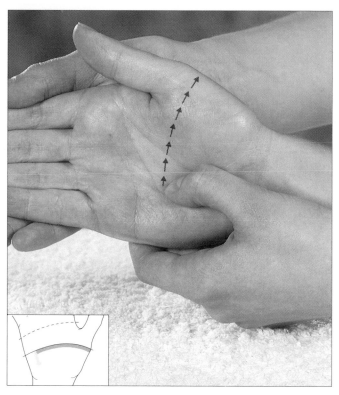

**11** Move your working thumb up slightly to the **ileo-caecal valve reflex** *(above)*. Gently rotate on this point before thumb-walking in a straight line up the **reflex to the ascending colon**. This lies in zones four and five and leads to the **hepatic flexure**. Press three to four times on this flexure before moving on.

**12** Alter the position of your working thumb so that it points towards your patient's right thumb *(above)*. Thumb-walk from the hepatic flexure, following the waist line, across the palm of the hand to the medial side of the thumb in zone one. You have now treated the **first part of the transverse colon**.

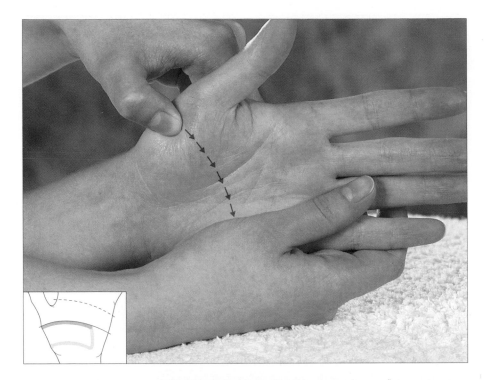

**13** The **remainder of the transverse colon** is found on the left hand *(right)*. Support the patient's hand with your right hand, place your working thumb just below the waist line in zone one. Following the waist line, thumb-walk across the palm of the patient's hand to the splenic flexure in zone five.

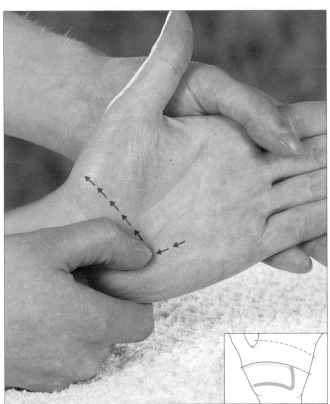

**14** Change over hands *(above)* and gently press over the splenic flexure with your right thumb. Then thumb-walk down the **descending colon** in zones four and five to the **sigmoid flexure**. Apply light pressure on that point. Continue across the **sigmoid colon reflex area**.

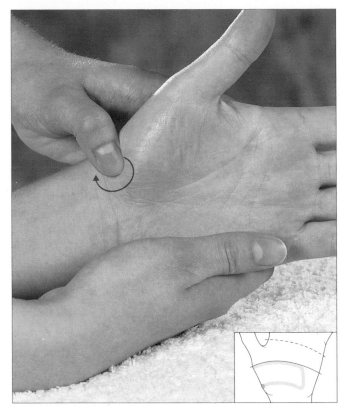

**15** Follow a straight line across all five zones on the palm of the hand until you reach the **reflex to the rectum and anus**, in zone one *(above)*. Then change hands and, supporting your patient's hand with your right hand, with your left thumb gently rotate on that point.

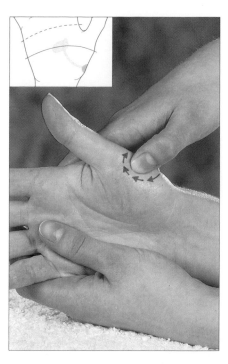

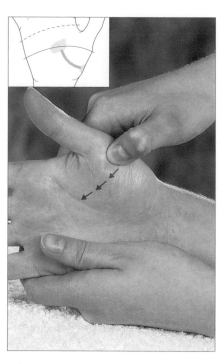

**16** To locate the **reflex for the bladder** *(far left),* find the point on the medial aspect of your patient's right thumb, midway between the head of the metacarpal and the wrist joint. Approximately the size of your thumbnail, it extends from the palm of the hand round to the back of the hand. Use the outer edge of your right thumb to walk around this area.

**17** Keep your working thumb positioned on the medial part of the bladder reflex *(left)* in readiness to treat the **reflex to the ureter tube**. This reflex extends upwards from zone one, across zone two, terminating just below the waist line in zone three where it joins the reflex to the right kidney. Thumb-walk up and across the hand to that point.

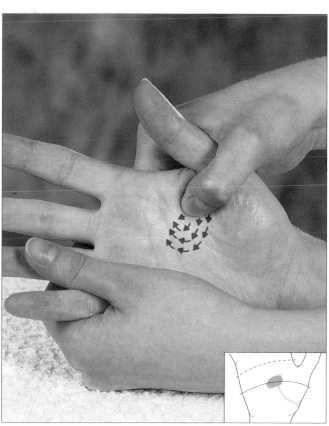

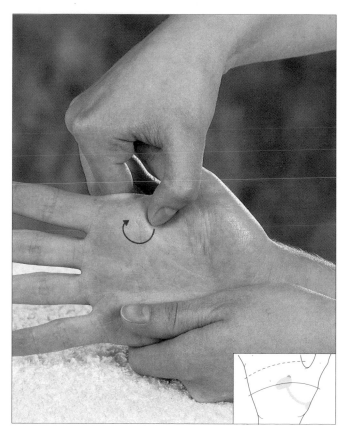

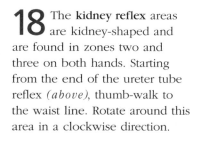

**18** The **kidney reflex** areas are kidney-shaped and are found in zones two and three on both hands. Starting from the end of the ureter tube reflex *(above)*, thumb-walk to the waist line. Rotate around this area in a clockwise direction.

**19** The **reflex to the right adrenal gland** is found just above the waist line in zone two *(above)*, close to the kidney reflex. Rotate on this point with your thumb in a clockwise direction. The left adrenal gland reflex is found on the left hand.

# Lower body reflexes

The reflexes to the lower body are often included in the description of abdominal reflexes, since they relate to organs found in the abdomen. However, none of them has any digestive function. Furthermore, with the exception of the sciatic nerve they are all found on the lateral and medial side of the feet and hands. Therefore treatment of these reflexes follows treatment of the reflexes located on the soles of the feet or the palms of the hands. The lower body reflexes consist of the sciatic nerve, sacro-iliac joint, pelvic muscles, knee, hip and reproductive organs of both the male and the female. They are important for chronic ailments associated with these areas. The reproductive reflexes can be tender and therefore should always be treated gently. Great care should also be exercised with the reproductive organs during the first sixteen weeks of pregnancy. These should not be treated if there is a history of miscarriage.

### Sciatic nerve

The sciatic nerve is the largest nerve in the body and supplies all the muscles of the legs and feet. It arises from the sacral plexus, runs from the spine across the buttocks, and down the back of each leg. Just above the knee, it divides into two branches which supply the lower leg. Pressure exerted on the sciatic nerve – often caused by a 'slipped disk' – produces sciatica, a burning pain radiating through the buttocks and down the back of the thigh. Working with the sciatic reflex can help relieve lower back pain.

### Sacro-iliac joint

This is an important joint transmitting the weight of the body, through the vertebral column, via the pelvis to the lower limbs. It is formed by the sacrum and the ilium and has very little movement. The reflex for this joint is important in cases of sciatica and for lower back or hip problems.

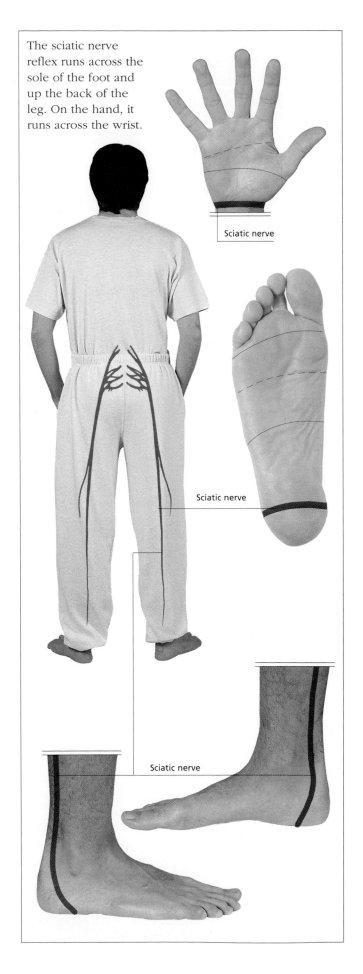

The sciatic nerve reflex runs across the sole of the foot and up the back of the leg. On the hand, it runs across the wrist.

Sciatic nerve

Sciatic nerve

Sciatic nerve

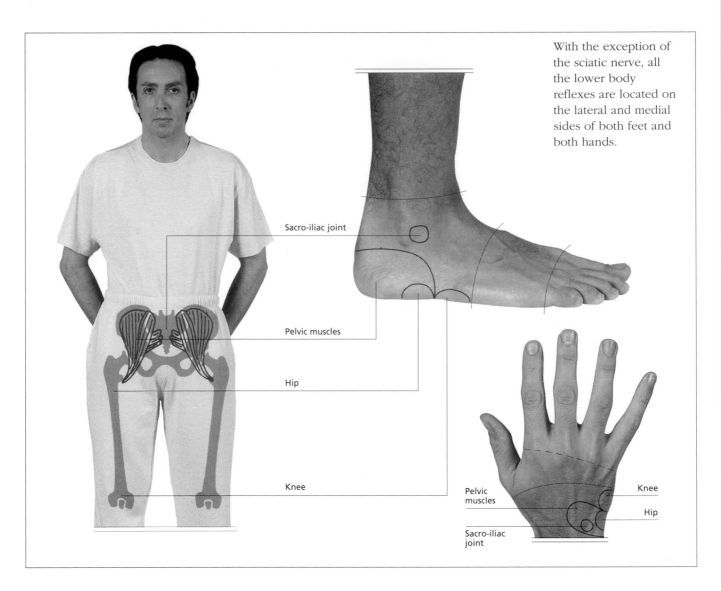

With the exception of the sciatic nerve, all the lower body reflexes are located on the lateral and medial sides of both feet and both hands.

Sacro-iliac joint

Pelvic muscles

Hip

Knee

Pelvic muscles

Knee

Hip

Sacro-iliac joint

## Pelvic muscles

The pelvis is continuous with the abdominal cavity. It is a big funnel-shaped ring of bone formed by the sacrum and coccyx, the pubic bones and the ischium. In all humans, the pelvis joins the legs to the spine in such a way as to maintain the upright position. In a woman, the pelvis also serves to hold and protect the reproductive organs: in the cavity of the pelvis lie the two ovaries. When a baby is born, it has to pass through the hole in the pelvis. In men this is small and flat, but in women it is round and the size of a baby's head The muscles related to this part of the body form the pelvic floor, and support the bone structure. The most important of these is the levator ani. The pelvic muscles reflex is important for lower back pain and problems related to the hips and pelvis.

## Hip

The hip is a major weight-bearing joint and is located where the pelvis meets the femur (thigh bone). It is a ball-and-socket joint, with a strong capsule surrounding it for strength. This reflex is important for back pain and for hip disorders such as arthritis.

## Knee

The knee is the largest joint in the body and is susceptible to most of the common joint disorders. Stability of the joint depends on the strength and tone of the quadriceps muscles on the front of the thigh, which hold the joint in position. The knee reflex is important for various forms of arthritis, including bursitis, rheumatoid arthritis and osteoarthritis of the knee, and any other problems that may be connected to this part of the body.

The reflexes to the male and
female reproductive organs are
found across the top of the foot,
and across the wrist on the
hands. The uterus or prostate
reflex is located on the medial
side of the foot and hand.
The ovaries or testes reflex is
located on the lateral side of
the foot and hand.

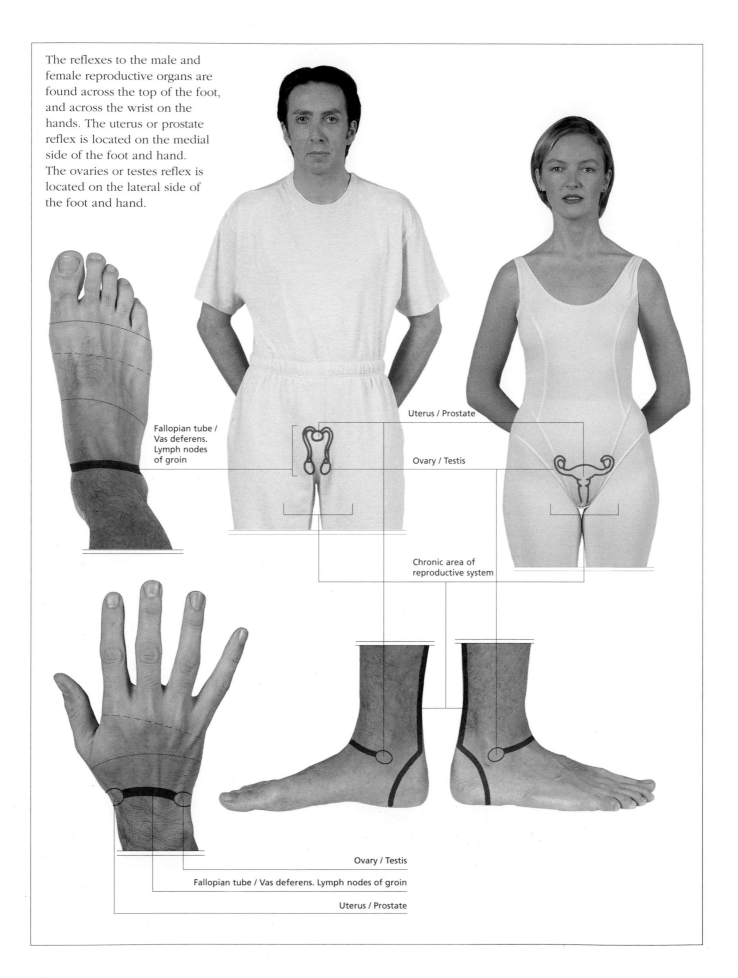

Fallopian tube /
Vas deferens.
Lymph nodes
of groin

Uterus / Prostate

Ovary / Testis

Chronic area of
reproductive system

Ovary / Testis

Fallopian tube / Vas deferens. Lymph nodes of groin

Uterus / Prostate

## Testes and vas deferens

The male sex glands or testes lie in the scrotal sac, just below the abdomen. This vulnerable position is necessary because the formation of spermatozoa requires a temperature slightly lower than that found in the abdomen. Each gland is attached to the body by a single spermatic cord composed of the vas deferens, or sperm duct, and a number of nerves and blood vessels.

The endocrine part of the testes are composed of clumps of cells that secrete the male hormone, testosterone. They also produce small amounts of the female hormone called oestrogen. The testes are under the control of the hypothalamus and the anterior pituitary gland, and do not develop until puberty.

The sperm that each testicle produces remains in a coiled tube, the epididymis, for approximately three months. After this time the sperm, now mature, passes into the vas deferens and seminal vesicles for storage. There, it swims in the seminal fluid, the volume of which depends on adequate testosterone. If the sperm is not ejaculated with the seminal fluid, it will disintegrate and be reabsorbed into the body.

## Prostate

The prostate gland comprises three major lobes, which surround the urethra at the point where it leaves the bladder. It is intimately associated with the lower urinary tract.

If it becomes enlarged in later life, it can press on the urethra, eventually closing it and making it impossible to pass urine. When this occurs, surgical intervention is needed. The lobes of the prostate are tubular, with muscles that squeeze their secretions into the urethra, particularly during sexual intercourse.

The main disorders that can affect the prostate are enlargement, infections and growths. These can be helped by working the reflex to this gland.

## Ovaries, uterus and fallopian tubes

The two ovaries and the uterus which lie in the lower part of the abdomen are the main female organs of reproduction. The ovaries, part of the endocrine system, are located on either side of the uterus, and each is connected to it by a small tube called the fallopian tube. Like the testes, the ovaries have two functions: to produce ova, or female egg cells, and to produce hormones that change a girl's body into that of a woman and prepare the uterus for pregnancy. The ovaries waken to activity at puberty through stimulation by the gonadotropins – the hormones secreted by the pituitary gland. In turn, the developing ovarian follicle secretes oestrogen responsible for enlarging the breasts, and for the uterus, the vagina and the rest of the genital tract, at puberty. Halfway through the menstrual cycle another hormone, prompted by the rising levels of oestrogen, is secreted by the pituitary gland. Under its influence, the developing ovum is released from the ovary, causing the vacated follicle to secrete progesterone. This hormone changes the lining of the uterus in preparation for the eventual reception of a fertilized egg.

The uterus, into which the fertilized ovum becomes embedded, is a hollow, pear-shaped organ about 10 centimetres (4 in) long, lying between the urinary bladder and the rectum. At the lower end of the uterus is the cervix, the narrow, thick-walled neck which leads into the top of the vagina. After a forty-week gestation period, the fully developed baby enters the world by passing through the dilated cervix and out through the vagina. If pregnancy does not occur, the lining of the uterus breaks down and is discarded through the menstrual flow.

The reflex areas to the reproductive organs in both the male and female are important in cases of infertility, and for all problems associated with those parts of the body.

# Lower body reflexes on the feet

The remaining abdominal or lower body reflexes are not found on the soles but on the lateral and medial sides of both the left and the right foot. The exception is the sciatic nerve reflex, which crosses the sole of the foot and continues up the back of the leg, on either side of the Achilles tendon. The reflexes to the male and female reproductive organs – the uterus and the prostate gland – are also found along this tendon. These reflexes are important when working with chronic conditions related to these glands.

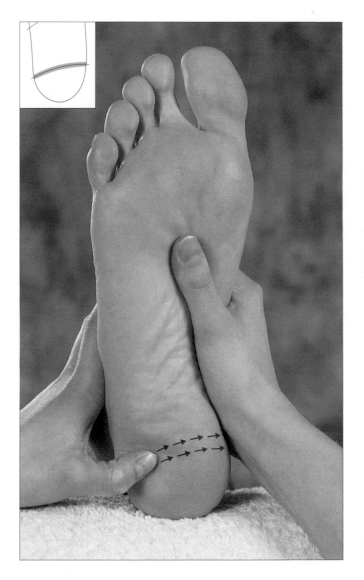

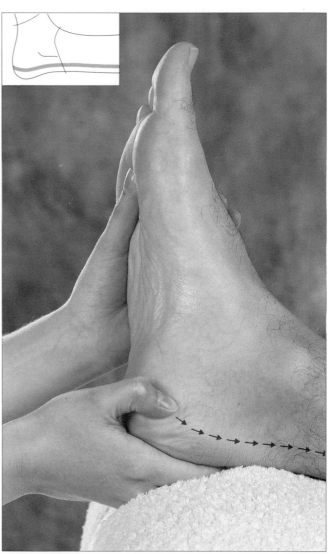

**1** To treat the **sciatic reflex**, wrap the fingers of your right hand around the foot *(above)*. For added support, hold the front of the foot with your working-hand fingers. Start about one-third down the lateral edge of the heel pad and thumb-walk two parallel lines across it.

**2** Holding the side of the foot and tilting it slightly with your left hand *(above)*, place your right thumb on the **medial aspect of the sciatic reflex** and thumb-walk back up the medial side of the Achilles tendon. Your working-hand fingers will support first the heel, then the leg.

**3** Reverse hands and wrap your right hand around the foot *(below left)*. From the outer edge of the sciatic reflex, thumb-walk up the lateral side of the Achilles tendon. When you reach the top of the tendon *(below right)*, place your fingers on the **medial side of the sciatic reflex** and work back down to the heel, gently squeezing the back of the leg.

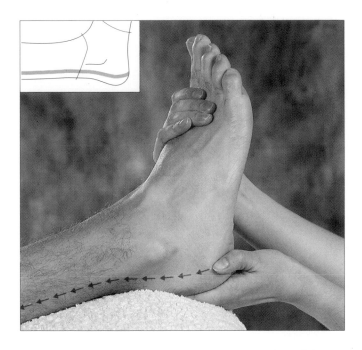

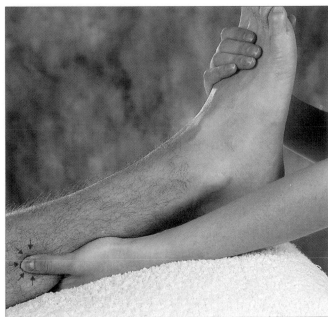

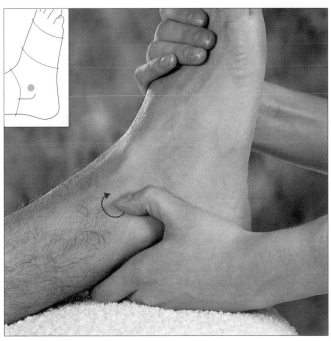

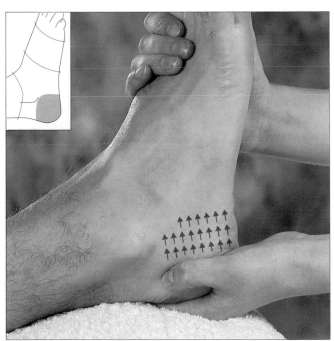

**4** Maintaining the supporting position of your right hand *(above)*, use the left thumb of your working hand to gently rotate around the **reflex area to the sacro-iliac joint**. You will find this in the dip which lies just in front of the ankle bone, in line with the fourth toe.

**5** The **reflex area to the pelvic muscles** lies on the lateral side of the foot, below the ankle bone. Hold the top of the foot with your right hand *(above)* and the heel with your left. Starting at the base of the ankle bone, walk your left thumb in vertical lines over the reflex area.

**6** Without changing the position of your hands, proceed to the reflex area for the hip and knee. These resemble two half moons and lie on the outer side of the foot, from the end of the metatarsal to a third of the way along the calcaneum. The half moon near the calcaneum is the **hip reflex** *(right)*. With the outer edge of your left thumb placed on the calcaneum, thumb-walk over this reflex.

**7** The half moon next to the hip reflex is the **reflex area to the knee** *(far right)*. Continue your thumb-walking until you have covered the whole reflex area.

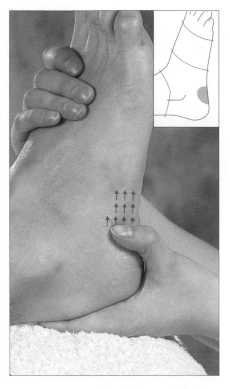

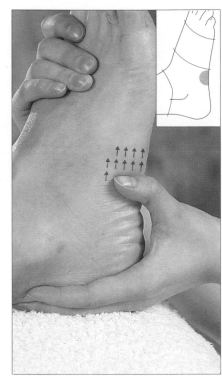

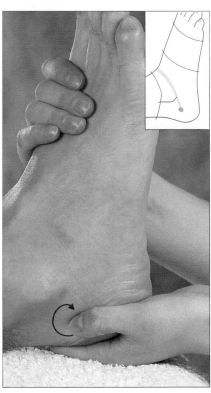

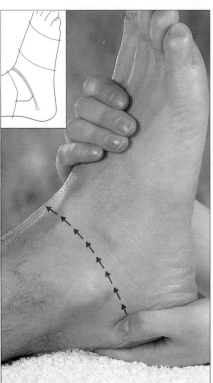

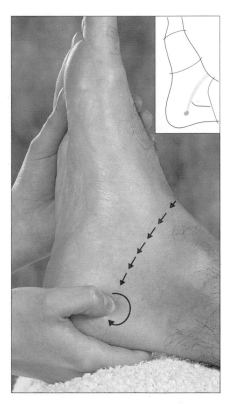

**8** Maintaining the same hand positions, tilt your patient's foot slightly to the right with your right hand *(above)*. The **reflex for the right ovary, or right testis**, lies midway between the outer ankle bone and the back of the heel. Rotate gently with your thumb.

**9** Thumb-walk across the top of the foot *(above)* to midway between the ankle bone and the back of the heel, on the inner side of the foot. This is the area that covers the **reflex to the right fallopian tube** or **the right vas deferens**. The corresponding left reflexes are found on the left foot.

**10** To treat the **uterus or prostate reflex**, you need to change the positions of your working and supporting hands *(above)*. Putting your right thumb over the reflex, slowly rotate your thumb around the area. This can be a tender area, so care is needed.

# Lower body reflexes on the hands

On the hands, the lower body reflexes are positioned across the back and front of the wrists, on both the medial and lateral sides of the hands. When you work with the reflex to the ovaries or testes, or the reflex to the uterus or prostate, always remember to apply only light pressure. If your patient experiences discomfort, apply gentle pressure only. On the hands, the reflex area for the sciatic nerve covers only the area across the wrist.

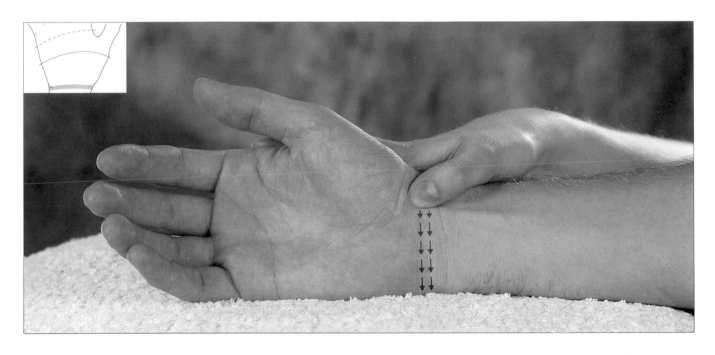

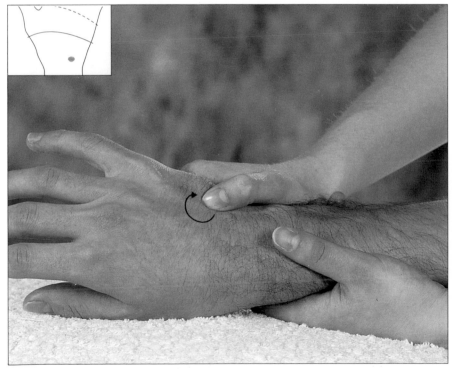

**1** The **reflex area to the sciatic nerve** is found across the wrist on the front of the hand *(above)*. Wrap your right hand around the hand of your patient and, with the outer edge of your right thumb, walk across the wrist from the medial side to the lateral edge. This reflex may be sensitive In some cases you may find it easier to support the patient's hand with your other hand.

**2** Turn over your patient's hand and rest the palm on the stool *(left)*. Wrap both your right and left hands around the patient's hand. Position the outer edge of your right thumb just above the wrist, in zones four and five. To treat the **reflex area to the sacro-iliac joint**, gently rotate on this point with your working thumb.

**3** Without altering the position of your left hand *(right)*, place the outer edge of your right thumb over the fifth metacarpal bone, on the top lateral side of your patient's hand. This is the point where the **pelvic muscles reflex** is located. The area corresponds to the muscles of the pelvic region on the right side of the body. Thumb-walk over the reflex area several times.

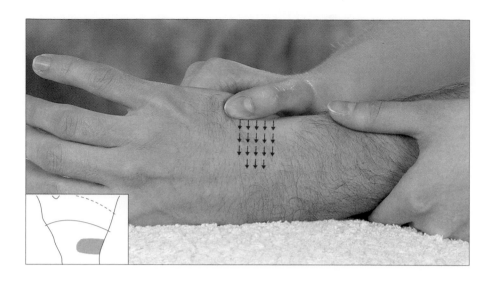

**4** Continue your treatment with the right hip and knee reflexes. These are both half moon-shaped and are found on the outer border of the back of the right hand, between the wrist and the waist line. The **hip reflex** *(right)* extends midway along from the wrist to the waist line. Use your left hand for support. Starting just above the wrist on the outer border of the hand, thumb-walk over one half-moon shape.

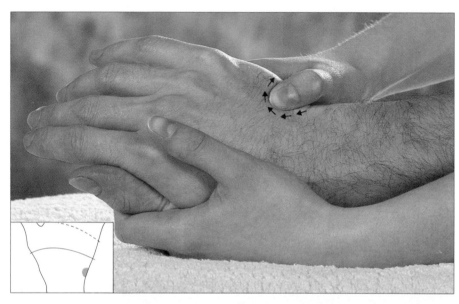

**5** The **knee reflex** *(below)* continues from the hip reflex to the waist line. Thumb-walk over the other half moon-shaped reflex which ends just below the waist line.

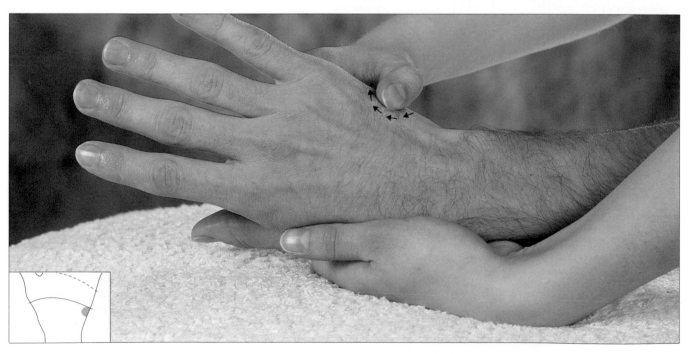

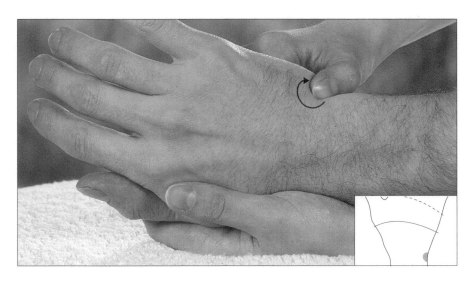

**6** From the knee reflex, move your working thumb to the wrist *(left)*, just below the point where you started your treatment to the hip reflex. This will bring you to the **right ovary reflex**, or the **right testis**. Gently rotate on this point for a few seconds. Apply only light pressure.

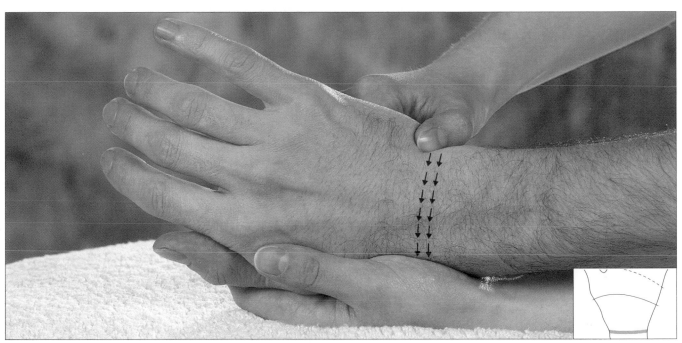

**7** From the right ovary or right testis reflex, thumb-walk across the wrist *(above)* to the medial side of the hand. This covers the area to the **right fallopian tube reflex** in a female or the **right vas deferens reflex** in a male.

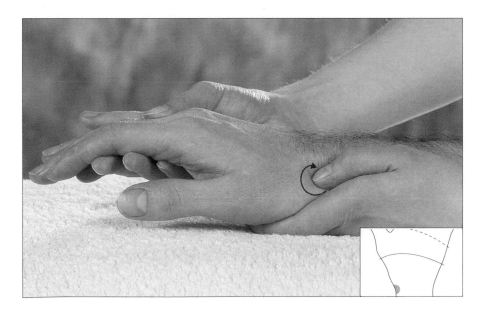

**8** On reaching the medial side of the hand *(left)* you will find a small hollow, slightly above the back of the wrist and in line with the web between the thumb and index finger. This hollow contains the **reflex area to the uterus** or **prostate**. Changing hands, wrap your right hand around your patient's hand and gently rotate your working thumb on this reflex.

# Reflexes on the
## top of the foot and the back of the hand

To complete a reflexology treatment, the remaining reflexes found on the top of the foot or the back of the hand are worked. These comprise the breasts, mid-back, and lymphatic system including lymph drainage. In the course of working with the breast reflex, it is possible to detect any cysts or lumps that may be present. When treating the lymph reflexes, puffiness in these areas may indicate swollen lymph nodes, which means that infection is present in the body. After completing treatment on these reflexes, finish it off by working with the simple relaxation techniques for the feet and hands described in Part One.

### Breasts

The essential function of the breasts is milk secretion and ejection. The milk secretion is due largely to the hormone called prolactin, with contributions from the progesterone and oestrogen hormones. Each breast consists of approximately fifteen to twenty groups of milk-producing glands, embedded in fatty tissue which gives the breast its characteristic shape. From each group of glands, a milk duct runs to the nipple. Around the nipple is a dark area, the areola, which contains small lubricating glands keeping the nipple supple. The breasts may enlarge as a result of the change in hormone levels, prior to menstruation and also during pregnancy. This reflex is important for disorders of the breast, such as benign or malignant lumps, and mastitis.

### Mid-back

The mid-back consists of the area between the tenth thoracic vertebra and the third lumbar vertebra. This reflex is beneficial for all back-related conditions. These include disc problems, muscular aches and strains, and various types of arthritis. When working with any of these disorders, it is advisable to give extra treatment to the spinal reflex as well as the mid-back reflex.

### Lymphatic system

The lymphatic system is widely distributed within the body. It consists of the lymph glands, or nodes, that are found principally in the neck, armpits and groin, and the small vessels that link them, the lymphatics. These contain a watery fluid, called lymph. The lymph nodes secrete very large numbers of lymphocytes, a type of white blood cell, which produce antibodies against recurrent infections. These nodes act as barriers to the spread of infection through the lymphatic vessels. The lymph carries nutrients and oxygen from the blood to every cell in the body, and drains back into the bloodstream through the lymphatic system. If there is a blockage in the flow of lymph, swelling (oedema) results. The reflex points for all of the lymph nodes are found on the top of the feet and the back of the hands. These include the upper lymph nodes and the lymph nodes to the axilla or armpit, the breast, the abdomen, the pelvis and the groin. These reflexes are important in cases of infection. They also help maintain a healthy lymphatic system to protect the body from disease.

### Lymph drainage

After you have finished treating the lymphatic system, complete this section by working on the lymph drainage reflex. This is found between the big toe and the second toe on the foot, and between the thumb and index finger on the hand.

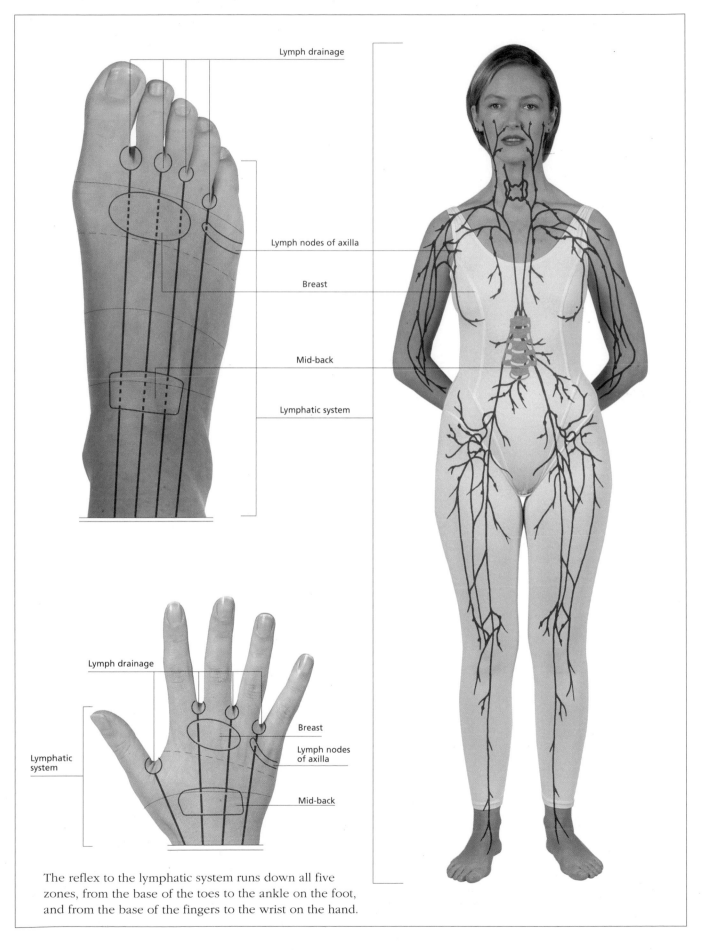

Lymph drainage

Lymph nodes of axilla

Breast

Mid-back

Lymphatic system

Lymph drainage

Lymphatic system

Breast

Lymph nodes of axilla

Mid-back

The reflex to the lymphatic system runs down all five zones, from the base of the toes to the ankle on the foot, and from the base of the fingers to the wrist on the hand.

95

# Reflexes on the top of the foot

The remaining reflexes found on the top of the foot are for the breasts, the mid-back and the lymphatic system. These reflexes are positioned between the base of the toes and the top of the ankle. In elderly people, the veins around the sides and over the top of the foot are sometimes prominent. If you encounter this, take the utmost care and work very gently over these areas to avoid bruising. When you work on the breast reflexes, feel for any abnormalities, since lumps or cysts in the breasts can be detected in the course of treatment. If that is the case, suggest that your patient seek medical advice.

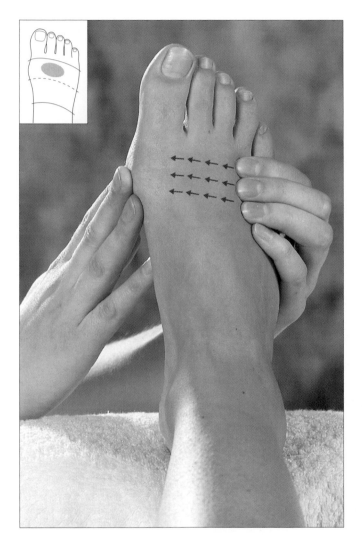

**1** The **breast reflex** is found in all five zones on the top of the foot and covers the area between the base of the toes and the diaphragm. Support the foot with your right hand (*above*). Place your left thumb on the sole, and with your next three fingers on the top of the foot, walk horizontally across this reflex.

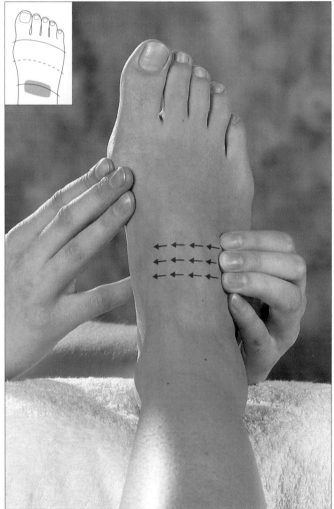

**2** Slide your working hand down the foot (*above*) to the **mid-back reflex**, which is found just below the waist line. Finger-walk horizontally across all five zones to just above the ankle. The thumb of your working hand should remain resting on the sole of the foot, behind your working fingers.

**3** Begin treating the lymphatic system *(right)* with the **reflex to the lymph nodes** of the right armpit, positioned just below the shoulder reflex. With the index finger of your left hand over this reflex, and your thumb on the sole of the foot, slowly rotate for a few seconds.

**4** The **reflex areas to the rest of the lymphatic system** are on the top of the foot *(below)*, from the webs of the toes to the ankle bone. Support the sole of the foot with your left hand. From the web between the first and second toe, thumb-walk down zone one. Repeat for all the other zones.

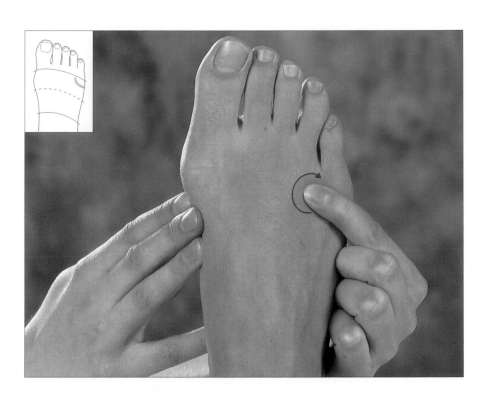

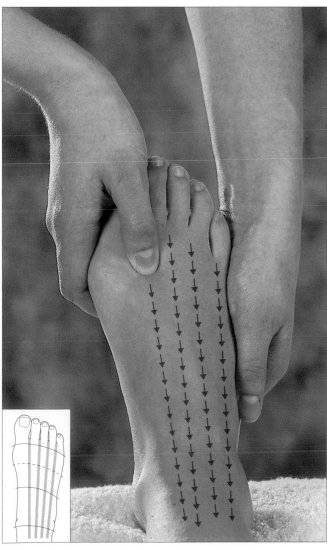

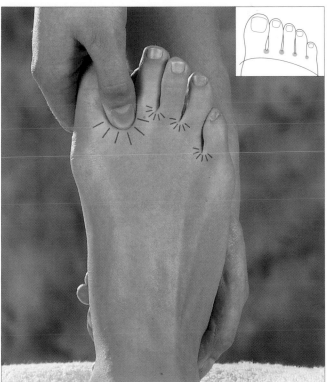

**5** The **reflex areas for lymph drainage** are found on the webs between the toes *(above)*. The most important of these is the web between the first and second toe. Support the foot with your left hand, and with the thumb and finger of your right hand, pinch and slide off each toe web.

97

# Reflexes on the back of the hand

On the back of the hand are found reflexes to the breast, the mid-back as well as the lymphatic system. The reflex areas to the upper lymph nodes are just below the webs between the fingers. Those to the abdomen are found below the diaphragm line in all five zones; for the pelvis and groin they are across the back of the wrist. When you work on the back of the hand, be careful over areas where there are prominent veins. Because the back of the hand works with the lymphatic system, it is important in building defence to infection.

1 The **breast reflex area** *(right)* is found above the diaphragm line and covers all five zones. Supporting the patient's hand with your left hand, place your working thumb on the knuckle of the little finger. Thumb-walk in horizontal lines across the right breast reflex to the diaphragm line.

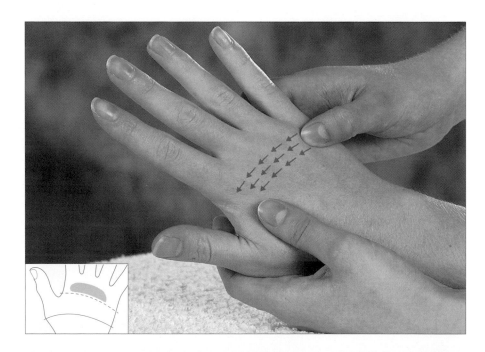

2 Retaining the position of your left hand, and using it as the supporting hand *(below)*, move your working thumb down to just above the waist line. Then thumb-walk horizontally across all five zones to the wrist. This covers the **reflex area to the mid-back**. If some discomfort is felt by your patient, apply only very light pressure.

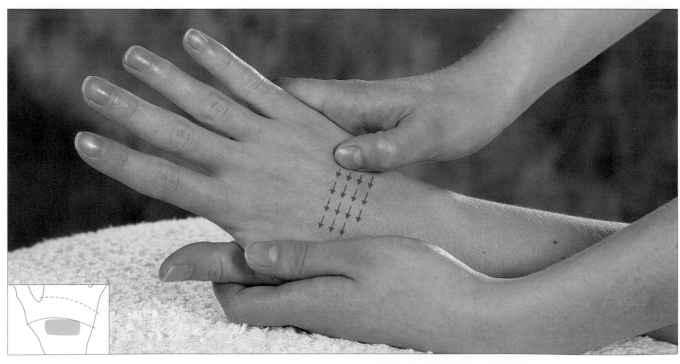

**3** Start your treatment of the lymphatic system *(below)* with the **lymph nodes to the right armpit**. The reflex for these lymph nodes is found over the knuckle of the little finger. Still using your left hand to support the patient's hand, thumb-walk around this area with your right hand.

**4** The **remainder of the lymphatic system reflex area** covers all five zones *(below right)*, from the webs of the fingers down towards the wrist bones. With either the right thumb or fingers, walk down the back of your patient's hand, between the metacarpal bones and over the wrist bones.

**5** The **lymph drainage reflex** is treated last. Using the thumb and finger of your right hand *(bottom)*, gently press and slide off the webs between the fingers. Start on the lateral side of the hand and finish between the thumb and index finger, on the main drainage point.

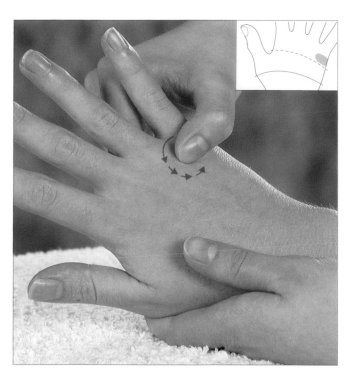

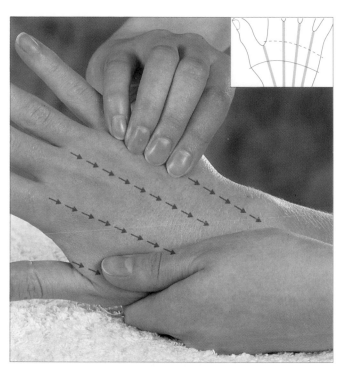

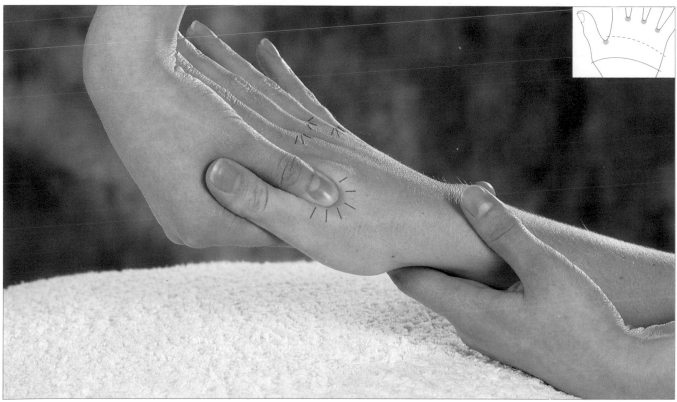

# Finishing the treatment on the feet

When you have worked all the reflexes on both feet, complete your treatment with foot massage. This relaxes the patient and stimulates energy flow. Massage techniques can be used on both feet prior to treatment, for people who are tense or under stress. There are five basic strokes: kneading, wringing, stretching, finger circling and stroking. These techniques are most effective when they are performed in this order. Follow your own judgement as to how much time you spend on these massage techniques.

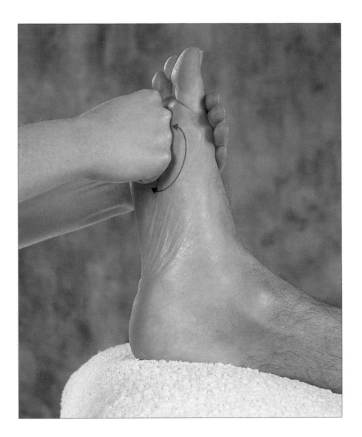

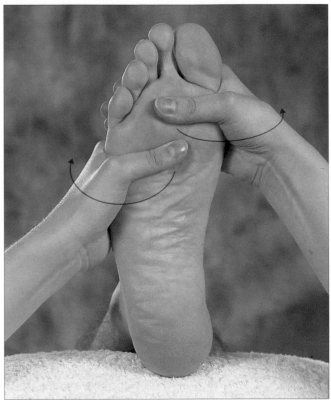

**1** Position one hand across the top of the foot *(above)* and place the clenched fist of the other on the sole of the foot. Kneading with both hands, make circular movements over the entire foot. This is wonderful both for stimulating energy and relaxing a person.

**2** Wrap your hands around the sides of the foot near the toes *(above right and right)*, with your thumbs on the sole. Then gently twisting your hands back and forth in a wringing action, work you way slowly down the foot until you reach the ankle.

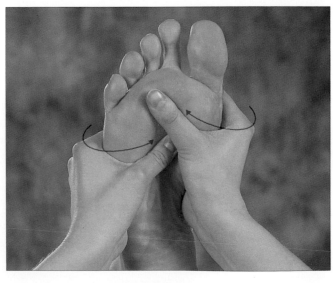

**3** Maintain both your hands in the same position *(below)*. Starting near the ankle, stretch the hands up towards the toes. Repeat several times. This action makes the whole body, especially the spine, feel as though it is being stretched upwards. It is good for people who work sitting at a desk all day.

**4** Place the fingers of both hands near the toes *(below right)*, and your thumbs on the sole of the foot. Work over the top and sides of the foot and around the ankle bones using tiny circular movements. This will stimulate the lymphatic system and is the most relaxing of the techniques.

**5** Complete your massage by stroking the foot *(bottom left)*. This stimulates the nerve endings and is a very soothing movement. Starting at the ankle, stroke the top and sides of the feet in a gentle upward movement with the fingers of both hands. Continue for as long as you think necessary.

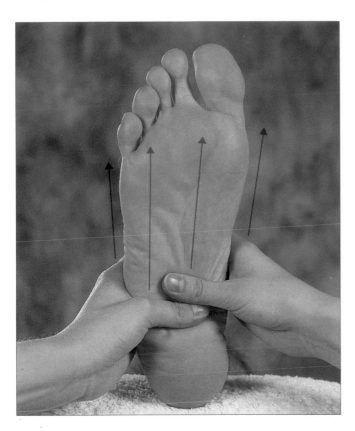

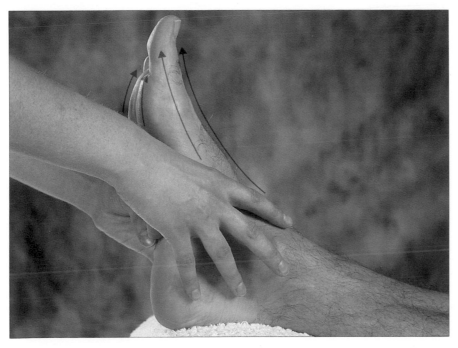

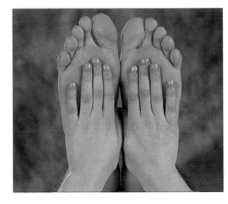

**6** When you have massaged both feet, press the palms of your hands against the soles of the feet *(above)*. Visualize a shaft of energizing golden light coming through the top of your head into your hands, and being transferred to your patient through his or her feet.

101

# Finishing the treatment on the hands

Make sure that you have worked every single reflex, on both hands. To finish the treatment, use the same massage techniques as for the feet, in the same sequence. They can also be used on both hands at the beginning of a treatment if the patient is stressed and tense. These techniques stimulate energy and also have a relaxing effect. When you are working on arthritic hands, take great care with the kneading, wringing and stretching movements. They could cause discomfort or damage to swollen or disfigured joints.

**1** Begin your massage with kneading *(above)*. Place one of your hands across the back of your patient's hand and the clenched fist of the other on the palm. Pressing both your hands into the patient's hand, make circular movements. This is an excellent technique for stimulating energy in the body and for strengthening and improving the hand's general structure.

**2** Wrap your hands around your patient's hand *(right)*, at the base of the fingers. Gently twist the patient's hand back and forth in a wringing action as you move slowly down towards the wrist. This action is beneficial for spreading out the bones in the hand, and it works similarly on the organs of the body.

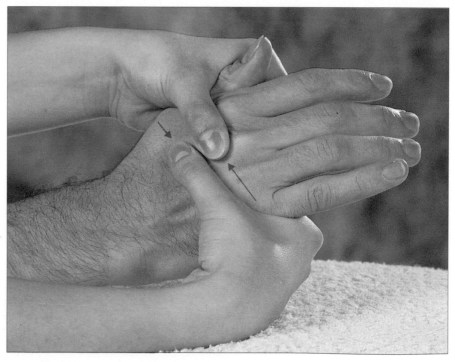

**3** Starting near the wrist, pull your hands up towards your patient's fingers *(below)*. Repeat this several times. This action works by making the body, especially the spine, feel as though it is being stretched upwards. It is extremely effective in helping to release any tension in the spine, muscles and organs.

**4** Position your fingers on the palm, and your thumbs on the back, of the patient's hand *(below right)*. Using tiny, circular movements, massage the back of the hand, starting from the base of the fingers and working your way down and around the wrist bones. This technique can be extremely relaxing.

**5** Using very gentle stroking movements over your patient's hands *(bottom left)*, massage both the palm and the back. Start at the wrist on the patient's palm and stroke lightly upwards with the fingers of both hands. Turn your patient's hand over and repeat the light upward strokes on the back.

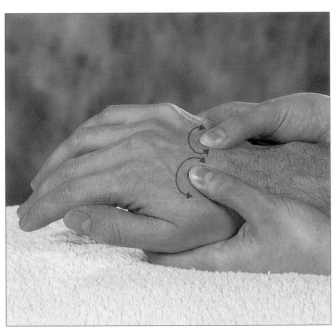

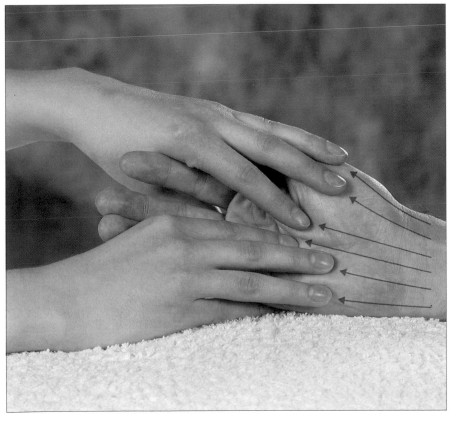

**6** When you have finished treating both hands, lay the palms of your hands against those of your patient *(above)*. Visualize a shaft of energizing golden light from the universe entering the top of your head and flowing into your hands. Imagine this light being transferred from your hands to your patient's hands, and eventually circulating throughout his or her body, to invigorate the whole being. Remain in this position for as long as you feel is necessary.

# Treating complaints with reflexology

Disorders are often detected during the course of a treatment. Some reflexes are found to be painful, thereby indicating specific problems requiring extra attention. However, reflexology is not a method of diagnosis. Remeber that if you encounter any serious conditions, you should advise your patient to consult a doctor.

Some of the complaints reflexology can benefit are given below, listed under the body system to which they are directly related. Causes and symptoms are described in order to help you understand the nature of the complaint, together with the reflexes requiring additional treatment (AT).

Remember that before you start treating any complaint specifically, a full reflexology treatment should be carried out.

## Spine

**Paralysis** The spinal cord is an important link between the brain and the rest of the body. It runs through the vertebral column, and is made up of bundles of nerves which transmit impulses between the brain and the physical body. This controls movements and the detection of sensations. If the spinal cord is damaged, numbness, weakness or paralysis occurs below the site of the injury.
AT: head, brain, spine; areas affected by the paralysis.

**Spinal meningitis** This is an inflammation of the meninges, the coverings of the brain and spinal cord, as a result of bacterial or viral infection. The symptoms include fever, headache, nausea, vomiting, a stiff neck and the inability to bear bright lights. This is a very serious disease and should receive prompt medical treatment. Reflexology can be of great help during the recovery period.
AT: head, brain, spine, lymphatic system and spleen.

## Head

**Epilepsy** This results from an electric problem in the brain's communication system. There are different forms of this disease, each with characteristic symptoms; but a generalized seizure is the most common. Here a person loses consciousness; the muscles of the entire body stiffen and start jerking uncontrollably. Sometimes a person blanks out but does not lose consciousness. When treating epilepsy, care should be taken because overstimulation could provoke an attack.
AT: brain, endocrine glands, spine and digestive system.

**Headaches** These can be caused by stress and tension creating strain on muscular tissues or blood vessels in the head or neck, or they may be the symptom of some underlying disorder. Other causes are excess alcohol, overeating, too little or too much sleep, a noisy or stuffy environment.
AT: head, spine, sinuses, eyes, neck, digestive system, liver and solar plexus.

**Migraine** This is an intense gripping pain confined to one side of the head. Its exact cause is not medically known. Susceptibility to this complaint tends to run in families. Sensitivity to some foods such as cheese or chocolate, or hormonal disturbances, may be contributory factors. Prior to an attack, abnormal tiredness can be felt. This is often followed by nausea, vomiting and an aversion to bright lights. Visual disturbances can also occur.
AT: head, solar plexus, spine, neck, sinuses, eyes, pituitary gland, thyroid gland, ovaries, digestive system and liver.

**Insomnia** The causes of insomnia – difficulty in sleeping, are numerous. They include stress, anxiety, eating too late in the evening or drinking too much tea or coffee. Those

suffering from this complaint need to look at their lifestyle in order to determine the cause.
AT: head, brain, solar plexus, adrenal glands, plus additional foot massage at the end of the treatment.

**Scalp complaints**  They include 'cradle cap', a form of eczema found on the head of babies; dandruff, an abnormal production of small flakes of dead skin on the scalp; psoriasis, overproduction of cells lacking in keratin (a hardening substance); ringworm, a fungus which infects the skin causing scaly, itchy patches to develop.
AT: head, endocrine glands, solar plexus and immune system.

**Sinusitis**  Sinusitis is an inflammation of the sinuses, or cavities in the bones of the face or skull. It usually develops as a result of a virus infection such as a cold, but it can also be caused by allergies. The symptoms are a blocked nose, a thick greenish-yellow discharge, a headache over one or both eyes and, if the maxillary sinuses are affected, pain in the cheeks.
AT: head, face, eyes, neck and lymphatic system.

**Catarrh**  Catarrh is a condition which affects the nose. Symptoms are a blocked nose, and discharge of either a clear or a thick opaque fluid. The most common causes are viral infections, allergies, nasal polyps, and an overdry atmosphere.
AT: head, face, neck and lymphatic system. If a food allergy is suspected, pay special attention to the digestive system reflexes.

## Eyes

**Cataract**  A cataract is loss of transparency of the lens of the eye, produced by the gradual clouding of the jelly-like substance that forms the lens This process blocks or distorts light entering the eye, thereby reducing vision. The most common cause is deterioration of the lens in old age. In advanced cases, the lens may become white and opaque.
AT: head and eyes.

**Conjunctivitis**  This is an inflammation of the transparent membrane that lines the eyelids and the white of the eyes. It can be caused by an infection or an allergy. The symptoms are bloodshot and sore eyes, and a discharge of pus and itchiness if it is caused by an allergy.
AT: eyes, head and lymphatic system.

**Glaucoma**  Glaucoma is an increase of pressure within the eye. When the fluid which continuously circulates within the eyeball is unable to drain away, then pressure within the eyeball increases. The symptoms are blurred vision, pain and redness in the eye. A severe attack can cause headaches and vomiting. This condition should receive urgent medical treatment. Reflexology can help during the recovery stage.
AT: head, spine, eyes and solar plexus.

## Ears

**Tinnitus**  This is a medical term for a buzzing, ringing or roaring sound in the ear heard only by the sufferer. The sound may be intermittent or continuous. There are numerous.causes for this condition
AT: ears, eustachian tube, head, neck, spine and solar plexus.

**Acute infection of the middle ear**  This can be either a viral or bacterial infection. It causes the eustachian tube, which connects the middle ear cavity with the back of the nose, to become swollen and blocked. In a bacterial infection, pus will form in the middle ear cavity. This disorder can develop after a cold or an infection related to the nose or throat. The symptoms are severe stabbing pain in the ear with the sensation of its being blocked, sometimes accompanied by temperature and some loss of hearing.
AT: ears, eustachian tube, face, neck, spine, solar plexus and lymphatic system.

## Neck

**Tonsillitis**  The two tonsils which lie at the back of the throat belong to the lymphatic system. The tonsils guard the entrance to the respiratory and digestive systems. Tonsillitis is caused by a bacterial or viral infection. It starts with a sore throat, difficulty in swallowing, and the tonsils become large and inflamed. This may be accompanied by a fever and cough. Glands on either side of the neck may swell and become tender.

AT: throat, neck, head, spleen and lymphatic system.

### Thyroid

**Simple goitre**  This is the name given to an enlarged but normally functioning thyroid gland. The most common cause is a lack of iodine in the diet. The symptom is a lump which develops and which can be seen and felt at the front of the neck.

AT: thyroid gland, neck, pituitary gland, adrenal glands and reproductive glands.

**Hypothyroidism**  This is the name given in the case of an underactive thyroid gland. This may be caused by a lack of iodine in the diet, or disorders of the pituitary gland. The most usual symptoms are a slowing down of the body processes.

AT: endocrine glands, especially the thyroid gland and the pituitary gland, and the spine.

**Thyrotoxicosis**  This is overactivity of the thyroid gland, causing a generalized speeding up of all chemical reactions in the body and affecting the mental as well as the physical processes. The symptoms are agitation, raised body temperature, an increased heart rate, diarrhoea, loss of weight, wasting muscles, ceased or scanty menstruation, and staring and protruding eyes.

AT: endocrine glands, eyes and reproductive glands.

## Shoulder

**Frozen shoulder**  This normally starts with a trivial injury or minor problem. The normal range of movement in the shoulder and arm is impaired because of stiffness and pain. If untreated, symptoms can worsen over a period of time.

AT: shoulder, arm, neck, upper spine and solar plexus.

## Chest

### Lungs

**Asthma**  This is a condition marked by attacks of breathlessness, and is produced by contraction of the wall muscles of the bronchi. The causes of asthma are varied and include allergies, drugs and various emotional or psychological upsets.

AT: lungs, bronchial tubes, heart, diaphragm, solar plexus and digestive system.

**Bronchitis**  This is an inflammation of the main air passages of the lungs and can be either acute or chronic. Acute bronchitis usually clears up in a few days, but with chronic bronchitis, the bronchial inflammation persists and gradually worsens. The main symptoms are a cough which brings up phlegm, breathlessness, wheezing, temperature and pain in the upper chest.

AT: lungs, bronchial tubes, throat, diaphragm, heart, solar plexus, and lymphatic system.

### Breasts

**Mastitis**  This is an inflammation of the breast which can occur prior to menstruation or can be caused by a bacterial infection. The symptoms are a painful breast to touch; the glands in the armpit may also be tender. A bacterial infection causes the temperature to rise.

AT: breast, lymphatic reflexes, arm and adrenal glands.

**Breast cancer**  This is a malignant tumour which develops in one or both breasts. At first it remains localized, but if not detected and treated it starts to spread, via the bloodstream and the lymphatic system, to other parts of the body. The cause is unknown. The symptoms are a breast lump which may or may not be painful. There may also be a dark coloured discharge from the nipple, or the nipple may become indented. If a lump is detected in the breast, medical advice should be sought immediately.

AT: breast, lymphatic system, pituitary gland, thyroid gland and lungs.

### Heart

**Angina** This is a condition in which the muscular wall of the heart becomes temporarily short of oxygen due to coronary artery disease, high blood pressure or, in a few instances, diseased heart valves. The main symptom is pain in the centre of the chest which can spread to the throat, upper jaw, back and left arm. Sometimes, difficulty in breathing, sweating, nausea and dizziness occur.
AT: heart, lungs, diaphragm, solar plexus and adrenal glands.

## Upper abdomen

**Tension or stress** The cause and symptoms of this condition can be many. To eradicate stress, the cause has to be found. Reflexology can be of tremendous help by inducing relaxation.
AT: solar plexus, heart, lungs, adrenal glands, plus additional massage to the feet at the end of treatment.

### Liver

**Hepatitis** This is an inflammation of the liver and, depending on the virus responsible, is called hepatitis A, B or C. Hepatitis A is spread through food or water contamination. Hepatitis B and C are spread by infected blood or through sexual activities. The more usual symptoms are loss of appetite, nausea, jaundice and in severe cases, liver failure. The blood of someone with hepatitis B or C is highly infectious.
AT: liver, lymphatic system, stomach, small and large intestines.

### Stomach

**Gastric ulcer** This is caused either by excess acidity created by the digestive juices, or by a type of bacteria which damages the protective mucus covering the stomach, thereby enabling the acid and enzymes to attack the stomach lining. The main symptom is a burning, gnawing pain throughout the upper part of the abdomen.
AT: stomach, small and large intestines.

**Indigestion** This is a term used to describe any complaint related to eating. Symptoms are distension of the abdomen, heartburn, nausea, or a taste of acid in the mouth.
AT: stomach, small and large intestines, diaphragm and solar plexus.

### Pancreas

**Diabetes mellitus** This is caused by a deficiency or total lack of insulin production by the pancreas. The result is a low absorption of glucose by the cells and liver and a high level of glucose in the blood. The symptoms are frequent urination, frequent thirst, a feeling of tiredness, leg cramps, reduced resistance to infection and sometimes blurred vision. If a person is taking insulin for this condition, it is important that they measure their blood sugar regularly when receiving reflexology treatment, as this may stimulate the pancreas.
AT: pancreas, pituitary gland, eyes, adrenal glands and kidneys.

### Adrenal glands

**Addison's disease** This is caused by the gradual decrease of steroid hormones that are produced by the outer layer of the cortex of the adrenal glands. The most common cause is destruction of the cortex by the body itself, due to an autoimmune problem. The usual symptoms are loss of weight, tiredness, weakness, anaemia, bouts of diarrhoea or constipation and a darkening of the skin.
AT: adrenal glands, pituitary gland, digestive system and all the reflexes of the lymphatic system of the body.

### Kidneys

**Nephritis** This is an inflammation of the kidney due to a bacterial infection. The symptoms are frequent urination, lower back pain, oedema and generally feeling unwell.
AT: kidneys, ureter tube, bladder and lymphatic system.

**Kidney stones** These may result from an excessive amount of calcium in the urine, and vary in size. If a stone is too large to pass down the ureter tube it may not present any problems, but smaller stones can cause renal colic, nausea and increased urination as they are eliminated via the ureter tube and bladder.
AT: kidneys, ureter tubes, bladder, lymphatic system, pituitary gland and adrenal glands.

## Lower abdomen

### Bladder

**Cystitis** This is an inflammation of the bladder usually caused by infection entering the bladder via the urethra. The symptoms are a frequent urge to urinate, with only a small amount of strong smelling, possibly blood-stained urine being passed. There may be discomfort in the lower abdomen and a slightly raised temperature.
AT: bladder, ureter tubes, kidneys, lymphatic system and prostate.

### Small intestine

**Crohn's disease** This is a chronic inflammation of the terminal part of the small intestine (ileum). The cause of the disease is unknown. The symptoms are cramps, abdominal pain (especially after eating), diarrhoea and a general sense of feeling ill.
AT: small and large intestines, adrenal glands and lymphatic system.

### Large intestine

**Constipation** This term refers to the failure of bowel movement, or the passage of hard stools, usually with some discomfort or pain. The most common cause is a diet low in fibre. Other causes include the use of certain medications, and psychological disorders such as severe depression.
AT: small intestine, large intestine, adrenal glands, liver and solar plexus.

**Cancer** In cancer of the large intestine, abnormal cells multiply and form either an ulcerous area that bleeds easily, or a blockage that hinders the passage of faeces. The main symptom is a change in the type of bowel movemen: either increased constipation or diarrhoea. Blood may also appear in the faeces, and there may be pain along with sensitivity in the lower part of the abdomen. This condition needs urgent medical attention.
AT: large intestine, small intestine, spleen, thymus gland and lymphatic system.

**Sciatica** This is a form of neuralgia caused by pressure on the sciatic nerve. The symptom is a burning pain which shoots through the buttocks, along the back of the thigh down towards the ankle.
AT: sciatic nerve and area up back of leg, lower spine, sacro-iliac joint, hip, knee and pelvic muscles.

### Ovaries

**Ovarian cyst** This is a sac full of fluid which grows on or near an ovary. The cause is unknown. It often produces no symptoms, but a firm, painless swelling may be noticed in the lower abdomen. If the cyst is large, it can press on the area near the bladder causing difficulty in emptying it. If hormone production is affected, irregular vaginal bleeding and an increase in body hair can ensue.
AT: ovaries, fallopian tubes, uterus and lymphatic system.

**Infertility** This term means a failure to conceive. There are many causes, one of the more common being faulty egg or sperm production, structural abnormalities of the reproductive tract, and psychological factors such as stress and anxiety.
AT: uterus or prostate, ovaries or testes, fallopian tubes or vas deferens, pituitary gland, thyroid gland and lymphatic system.

### Uterus

**Fibroids** A fibroid is a benign tumour of which develops either inside or outside the uterus. If the fibroid is large, symptoms can include heavy, prolonged and painful periods, a hard, painless lump in the lower abdomen, and difficult urination if the fibroid presses on the area near the bladder.

AT: uterus, ovaries, fallopian tubes and lymphatic system.

### Prostate

**Enlarged prostate** With age, small gristly nodules can develop on the prostate gland, enlarging its size and making it liable to obstruct the urethra and stop the flow of urine from the bladder. The symptom is a weak stream and in some cases, acute retention.
AT: prostate, bladder, kidneys and urethra.

### Testes

**Hydrocele** This is a swelling caused by the accumulation of a clear, thin fluid between the outer and inner layers covering the testes. There is usually no obvious cause for this condition but it can be brought about by inflammation or injury. The symptom is normally a soft swelling around the testicles.
AT: testes and lymphatic system.

### Anus

**Haemorrhoids** This condition is caused by the swelling of the varicose veins which lie under the mucous membrane lining the lowest part of the rectum and the anus. Haemorrhoids may occur during pregnancy, whenever there is persistent straining during the act of defecation, or through obesity. The main symptoms are pain and bleeding during defecation.
AT: rectum, large intestine, small intestine and solar plexus.

## Skin

**Psoriasis** This is a condition in which the speeding up of cell production results in abnormally low levels of keratin, the substance which gives the skin its hard surface. One of the causes can be mental stress. The symptoms are large or small raised pink patches on the skin, covered by white scales, most commonly found on the elbow, knees and scalp. In some cases the nails can be affected.
AT: the parts of the body affected plus adrenal glands, solar plexus, digestive system and pituitary gland.

**Eczema** This is an inflammation of the skin accompanied by itching, flaking, redness and tiny blisters. It may be due to allergies or it can be stress related.
AT: the parts of the body affected, plus the solar plexus, liver, digestive system, adrenal glands and kidneys.

# 3

# Taking reflexology further

T he information and techniques given in this section are intended for those who have mastered the art of reflexology and, preferably, have gained recognized qualification in this therapy.

The first part deals with the subtle anatomy. Every therapist should be familiar with this subject. Disharmony starts in the aura, or magnetic field, which surrounds us. If it is not dealt with at this level, it will manifest as disease in the physical body. Because the aura interpenetrates with the physical body, we automatically work with it when treating the feet and hands. This is how reflexology can be a preventive treatment.

The next part deals with the acupuncture meridians, which permeate the physical form. Each meridian starts or ends on one of the toes or fingers, and can therefore be traced on the hands and feet. When a reflex is painful for no apparent reason, it may be due to an imbalance in the meridian which runs through it. Knowledge of all the meridians provides the reflexologist with greater insight into the patient's health.

The last part combines reflexology with colour therapy. Colour fills and surrounds everyone. Disharmony in the aura is 'seen' as either an absence of colour, or wrong colours in the wrong places. The two therapies combine to remove energy blocks and, by introducing the right frequency into the body through the medium of colour, restore harmony. A great spiritual teacher once said that 'A mental colour treatment is an activity of great beauty and power in the higher planes, and is a great benefit and refreshment to the healer as well as the patient'.

Opposite *The healing colours of the universe flow through the sensitized body and hands of the therapist and are projected onto the reflex zones of the patient's feet.*

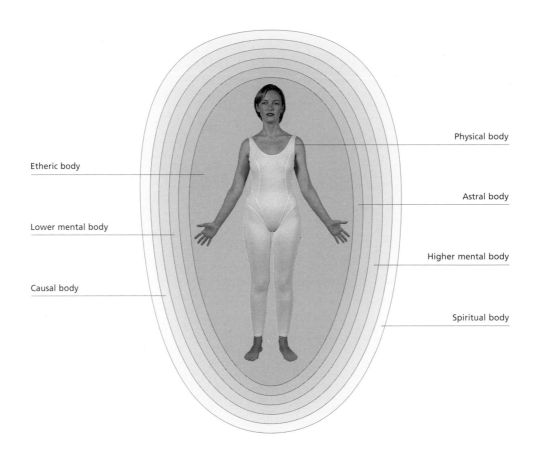

Etheric body

Lower mental body

Causal body

Physical body

Astral body

Higher mental body

Spiritual body

# The subtle anatomy

The subtle anatomy surrounding a person is known as the aura – or electromagnetic field. It is ovoid in shape. The widest part is around the head and the narrowest is under the feet. The aura is made up of seven layers or bodies. Each of these layers interpenetrates and works with the others. The layers consist of the physical, etheric, astral, lower mental, higher mental, causal and spiritual bodies.

The spiritual body is the outer layer of the aura and represents the divine or true self. It is the aspect of each individual which knows no beginning and no ending – the essence of that ultimate reality which we call God or Universal Consciousness.

Next lies the causal body. This contains the record of all our previous lives, plus the reason for our present incarnation. When we reincarnate, we bring with us the knowledge of the path that we have chosen to walk and

the challenges we have selected to meet. Unfortunately, from the moment of birth we are subjected to conditioning which makes us forget our life plan – like leaving the map behind and having to find our way without it.

The fifth layer is the higher mental body. It is at this level that we are able to get in touch with our intuition.

One of life's tasks is learning to listen to and trust this quiet inner voice, especially when using colour with reflexology. When we are able to tune in to our intuition, making the right decisions becomes easier, and this helps us to find and walk along our chosen path. Unfortunately, few people as yet have acquired this ability.

Above *Every person is surrounded by an aura, composed of seven auric bodies. Its width depends on spiritual growth.*

The fourth layer is the lower mental body. It is filled with constantly changing thought forms. Every thought that we – and the rest of humanity – have, creates a form or shape. If we think negative thoughts, they will attract other negative thought forms, and thereby amplify the original thought. In the same way, positive thoughts will attract positive thoughts. For this reason, it is most important to be aware of our negativity and endeavour to change it into positive thinking. This may be difficult at first, but with patience, practise and determination, it can be achieved.

The third layer is the astral body, which has a connection with our emotions. In highly emotional people, this layer is constantly fluctuating and therefore in a state of imbalance. As we walk into the next millennium and confront the challenges and changes that it will bring, it is important that we learn to master our emotions, and not let our emotions become the master of us.

Closest to the physical body – the first body – lies the etheric body. This layer is the blueprint for the physical body, and disintegrates with it at death. It is in the etheric body that disease starts and can be 'seen' or 'felt' as an accumulation of energy in the wrong place. If this is not eradicated, it will ultimately manifest itself as a disorder in the physical body. The etheric body contains the chakras and nadis. The nadis are energy channels and are connected with the nervous system. The chakras are energy centres, wheels of rotating energy which absorb prana, or life force, from the atmosphere, break it up, and distribute it through the nadis to the nervous system, endocrine glands and circulatory system.

## The major chakras

The etheric body contains seven major chakras, formed at the points where twenty-one lines of energy – or nadis – cross; and twenty-one minor chakras, where fourteen nadis cross. Acupuncture points are formed where seven nadis cross.

The twenty-one minor chakras are located in the body: one behind each eye; one in front of each ear; one midway along each clavicle; one lies close to the thymus gland; one above each breast; one in the palm of each hand; two connected with the spleen; one near the liver; one connected with the stomach; one related to the ovaries in a female and the testes in a male; one behind each knee and one on the sole of each foot.

Each of the seven major chakras is associated with one of the endocrine glands in the physical body. They are situated in line with the spine, and are also found on the spinal reflex on the feet and hands. Because of their association with the endocrine glands – which secrete their hormones directly into the bloodstream – it is important to locate and treat these major chakras during a reflexology session, especially if a person is suffering from a hormonal disease.

The seven major chakras are the base, the sacral, the solar plexus, the heart, the throat, the brow and the crown. Each of these centres contains all eight colours of the spectrum, but each radiates only one specific colour.

### The crown chakra

The crown chakra, or 'sahasrara', is situated just above the crown of the head. On the feet, it is found on the top of the big toes, and on the hands, it is positioned on the tops of the thumbs. It is symbolized as a thousand-petalled lotus, representing infinity. Its dominant colour is violet, but the dominant colours of the other six major chakras are reflected here and unite with the violet to form the white light of divine consciousness. The endocrine gland associated with this chakra is the pineal gland.

When this chakra functions to its full potential, spirituality is seen in a very personal way – that is, unrelated to any dogma. If it is awakened prematurely, by the use of hallucinatory drugs for example, then it can lead to epilepsy, coma and psychic maladjustment.

### The brow chakra

The brow chakra, or 'ajna', is situated at the centre of the brow between the two eyebrows. On the spinal reflex of the feet and

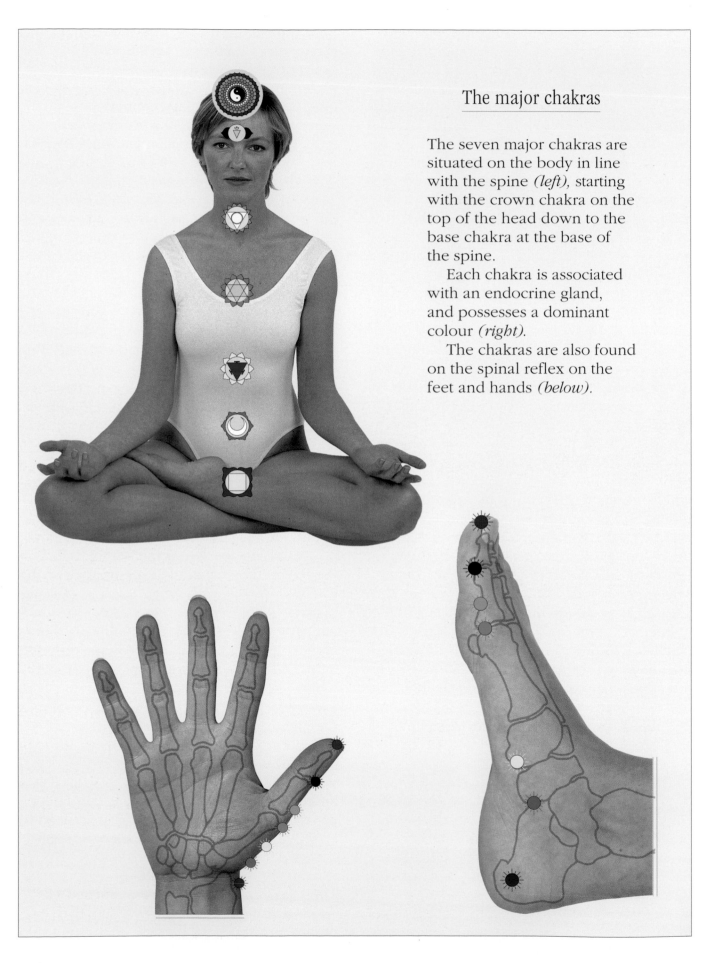

## The major chakras

The seven major chakras are situated on the body in line with the spine *(left)*, starting with the crown chakra on the top of the head down to the base chakra at the base of the spine.

Each chakra is associated with an endocrine gland, and possesses a dominant colour *(right)*.

The chakras are also found on the spinal reflex on the feet and hands *(below)*.

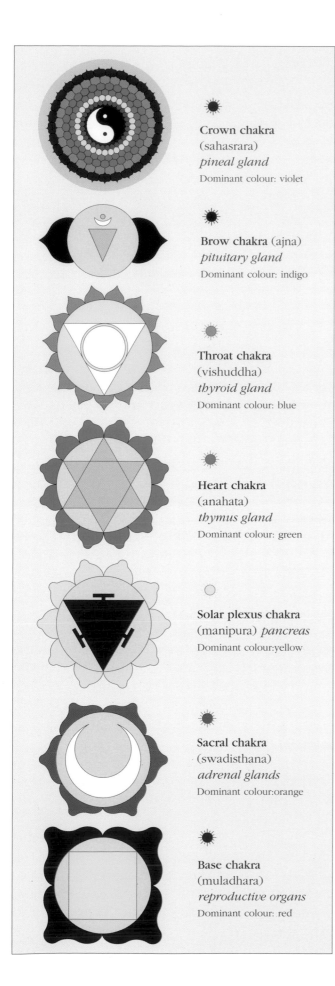

**Crown chakra**
(sahasrara)
*pineal gland*
Dominant colour: violet

**Brow chakra** (ajna)
*pituitary gland*
Dominant colour: indigo

**Throat chakra**
(vishuddha)
*thyroid gland*
Dominant colour: blue

**Heart chakra**
(anahata)
*thymus gland*
Dominant colour: green

**Solar plexus chakra**
(manipura) *pancreas*
Dominant colour:yellow

**Sacral chakra**
(swadisthana)
*adrenal glands*
Dominant colour:orange

**Base chakra**
(muladhara)
*reproductive organs*
Dominant colour: red

hands, it is found at the joint between the first and second phalanges. This chakra is often referred to as the third eye. When awakened, it brings the gifts of telepathy and knowing.

This chakra is depicted with two indigo lotus petals. These represent the ego self and the spiritual self; the rational and the intuitive mind. The dominant colour is indigo. Inside the two petals lies a circle containing a golden downward pointing triangle, above which sit a white crescent moon and a golden sun. It is at this centre that the masculine and feminine aspects of our being merge, initiating a spiritual awakening.

On the physical level, the brow chakra is related to the eyes, nose, ears and brain. The endocrine gland to which it is related is the pituitary gland. Instability in this centre leads to tiredness, irritability, confusion and rigid thoughts. Imbalances can lead to sinus problems, stress, neuritis and migraine.

### The throat chakra

The throat chakra, or 'vishuddha', is situated in the throat area, between the two clavicle bones. On the spinal reflex of the feet and hands, it is located halfway along the second phalanges. It is symbolized by a smoky blue lotus flower with sixteen petals. Its dominant colour is blue. The centre of the lotus is yellow and contains a white downward pointing triangle. At the centre of the triangle is a yellow circular band encompassing a white circle. This chakra is associated with the element of ether and the sense of hearing.

On the physical level, this chakra governs the nervous system, the female reproductive organs, the vocal cords and the ears. The endocrine glands linked with it are the thyroid and the parathyroids.

The throat chakra is the creative centre – especially of the spoken word. It is related to the female reproductive organs because after the menopause, the creative energies of the sacral chakra are transmuted to the higher creative energies of the throat centre. The exceptions are in women who have opted to take hormonal replacement therapy at the onset of the menopause.

Apart from the spoken word, this centre is used for singing. Music, especially when produced by the voice, is very therapeutic. Medieval Christian monastic infirmaries used music to help people in pain, to comfort the terminally ill and support a conscious death. In her book *The Luminous Wand*, Therese Schroeder-Sheker, a music therapist and professor of music at Regis University, Denver, USA, describes how the harp and voice are used to assist the entire process of dying in the home, hospital and hospice.

As this centre starts to function to its full potential, it brings with it the gift of telepathy and the knowledge of past, present and future. It also represents the bridge between the physical and spiritual realms. When a person 'crosses' this bridge, his or her energy patterns change. This inevitably brings about transformation in other spheres of life.

Imbalance in this chakra can lead to asthma, vertigo, allergies, anaemia, fatigue, laryngitis, sore throats and menstrual problems. It can also cause a tendency towards skin and respiratory problems.

### The heart chakra

The heart chakra, or 'anahata', is situated between the fourth and fifth thoracic vertebrae. On the spinal reflex of the feet, it is found at the joint of the metatarsal bone and second phalange. On the spinal reflex of the hands, it lies where the second phalange of the thumb joins the metacarpal bone.

It is symbolized by a green lotus with twelve petals, and its dominant colour is green. In the centre of the lotus is a smoky blue hexagram (as in the star of David). It is associated with the element of air and the sense of touch.

On the physical level, this centre is identified with the heart and circulatory system, the lungs and respiratory system, the immune system, and the arms and hands. The endocrine gland to which it is attributed is the thymus. This gland plays an important role in our immune system.

This is the centre through which we love. There are many kinds of love: selfish, demanding, possessive, constricting, tender and caring. The more this centre is functioning to its full potential, the more will we be capable of undemanding spiritual love. In a love relationship, it puts us in touch with our partner. It helps us to perceive the beauty and spiritual love in human beings, and acquire greater sensitivity and distance from material objects.

When this chakra is out of balance, it can lead to heart attacks, stomach ulcers, an unhappy emotional life, fear, bitterness and resentment.

### The solar plexus chakra

The solar plexus chakra, or 'manipura', is situated between the twelfth thoracic vertebra and the first lumbar vertebra. On the spinal reflex of the feet, it is located at the back of the cuneiform bone, just where it meets with the navicular bone. On the spinal reflex of the hands, it is found along the metacarpal bone. In Chinese philosophy it is called the triple heater, due to the heat generated during the process of digestion. In Japanese teachings it is called the 'hara', which means belly. This chakra is depicted as a bright yellow lotus with ten petals. At its centre is a downward pointing triangle, with a T-shaped projection on each of its three sides. Its dominant colour is yellow and it is associated with the fire element. It is the centre of vitality because it is where prana (the upward moving cosmic energy which pervades the upper part of the body) and apana (the downward moving energy which operates in the pelvic region) meet, generating the heat that is necessary to support life.

On the emotional level, this centre is connected to desire. It is very active in people who are highly emotional, or who lack confidence and courage.

On the physical level, the solar plexus chakra is concerned with digestion and absorption. It influences the glands, processes and organs such as the breath, the diaphragm, stomach, duodenum, gall bladder and liver. It is associated with the endocrine part of the pancreas, namely the islets of Langerhans.

When this chakra is not functioning well, a person may be subject to rapid mood swings, and may suffer from depression, introversion, lethargy, poor digestion, abnormal eating habits and skin problems. When it is functioning to its full potential, a deep and fulfilling emotional life is experienced.

### The sacral chakra

The sacral chakra, or 'swadisthana', is situated halfway between the pubis and the navel. On the feet, it is found where the navicular bone joins the calcaneum; on the hands, at the base of the metacarpal bone. This chakra is symbolized by an orange lotus with six petals. Its dominant colour is orange. Inside these petals lies a white crescent moon, symbolic of female receptivity. The moon is associated with the water element and affects the flow of fluids in the body.

This centre is connected with the emotions of fear and anxiety. The glands and organs which it influences are the skin, the reproductive organs, the kidneys, bladder, circulatory system and lymphatic system. The endocrine glands connected with it are the adrenals.

When this chakra is functioning to its full potential, it opens the intuitive and psychic powers. Malfunction may result in a woman being unable to reach orgasm during sexual union. In a man, it is manifest in premature ejaculation or the inability to achieve an erection. Other disorders which may occur are problems with the kidney, and bladder, the circulatory system, menstruation and the production of seminal fluids.

### The base chakra

The base chakra, or 'muladhara', is sometimes referred to as the root centre because it is positioned at the base of the spine. On the feet, it is found at the lower back edge of the calcaneum; on the hands, at the bulbous part of the radius.

It is symbolized by a deep red lotus flower with four petals. The lotus depicts spiritual unfolding because, from its base rooted in slime, it grows upwards through the opaque waters to flower in the sun and light of heaven. At the centre of the flower is a yellow square which represents the earth and its stability. The dominant colour radiating from the muladhara is red. It is associated with the earth, regulates the sense of smell, and is also the centre for physical energy and vitality.

This chakra affects the legs, feet, bones, large intestine, spine and nervous system. The endocrine glands associated with it are the gonads – the testes in a male and the ovaries in a female. I feel that this centre has greater influence over the testes, while the ovaries are influenced more by the sacral chakra.

When this centre functions to its full potential, a person is filled with strength and vitality and wants to live life to the full. When it is sluggish, energy levels are low and there is no enthusiasm for life.

## Treating the chakras

At the end of every reflexology treatment, all the chakras should be treated on the spinal reflexes of the feet or hands. When one of the chakras is out of balance it can affect the other six.

Remember that both reflexology and colour therapy are holistic therapies – treating the human being as a whole.

Begin with the right foot or hand. Work with the pivoting technique for five to ten seconds on each chakra. Start by the crown chakra and work to the base chakra. The reason why these centres are worked in this order is because energy rises from the base chakra. By working in this way, the pathway is cleared for the energy to rise unimpeded.

If there exists an imbalance in any of the chakras, some discomfort may be experienced by your patient.

---

### Caution

If the patient is in the first twelve weeks of pregnancy, treatment should only be undertaken by a qualified reflexologist.

---

# The acupuncture meridians

Acupuncture has its roots in classical Chinese medicine, which was based primarily on works ascribed to three legendary emperors. These were Fu Hsi (2900 BC), Shen Nung, known as the Red emperor (2800 BC), and Yu Hsiung, known as the Yellow emperor (2600 BC). Yu Hsiung is famous for his medical compendium, the Nei Ching. The section entitled Ling-Hsu, meaning spiritual nucleus, is the part which deals with acupuncture.

Ancient Chinese cosmology states that the universe was created through the interplay of nature's basic duality: the active, light, dry, warm, positive, masculine yang, and the passive, dark, cold, moist, negative yin. All things are a combination of these positive and negative energies. If the yin yang balance is maintained, good health, long life and a youthful physique will ensue. Disregard of this balance leads to illness.

The Chinese believed that the vital force, called ch'i (pronounced tchee), circulates in the body through meridians, travelling a set route between organs and systems. The meridians are either yin or yang depending upon which way ch'i flows. If it flows freely and correctly through each of the twelve meridians, then the body is kept in balance and in good health.

If illness occurs, there are five methods of treatment according to the Nei Ching: cure the spirit, nourish the body, give medications, treat the whole body and use acupuncture. This consists of inserting needles into specific points located on the meridians. The different techniques used to manipulate the needles, once inserted, either disperse or draw energy into a meridian.

The Chinese discovered that there is one continuous meridian circulating in the physical body. It divides into fourteen branches – or meridians. Each of these has an internal branch which penetrates the organ that it is connected with, and a surface branch. It is the surface branch which houses the acupuncture points and which is worked with during a reflexology treatment.

Only twelve of the fourteen meridians are deemed important. A specific organ is related to each of these, and gives it its name. Each meridian is coupled with a second meridian. Both complement each other in their yin and yang aspect, and both share the same element and its attributes. The two less important meridians are not normally used.

All the meridians are bilateral, which means that they follow the same pathway on both the left and the right side of the body. Since the feet and the hands mirror the entire body, they also mirror the twelve meridians. Six of these either terminate or start on the feet, and six terminate or start on the hands.

The Chinese also believed that physiological functions were based on the humoral system which consisted of five essential humours – elements – namely metal, earth, fire, water and wood. (The reason for this may have been the mysticism which surrounded the number five in China.)

As well as working with the yin and yang aspect of the meridians, the traditional

## Key to meridians

| | |
|---|---|
| ———— | liver *(yin)* |
| – – – – | gall bladder *(yang)* |
| ———— | heart *(yin)* |
| – – – – | small intestine *(yang)* |
| ———— | pericardium/circulation *(yin)* |
| ▪ ▪ ▪ ▪ | triple heater *(yang)* |
| ———— | kidney *(yin)* |
| – – – – | bladder *(yang)* |
| ———— | lung *(yin)* |
| ———— | large intestine *(yang)* |
| ———— | spleen/pancreas *(yin)* |
| | stomach *(yang)* |

# The meridians

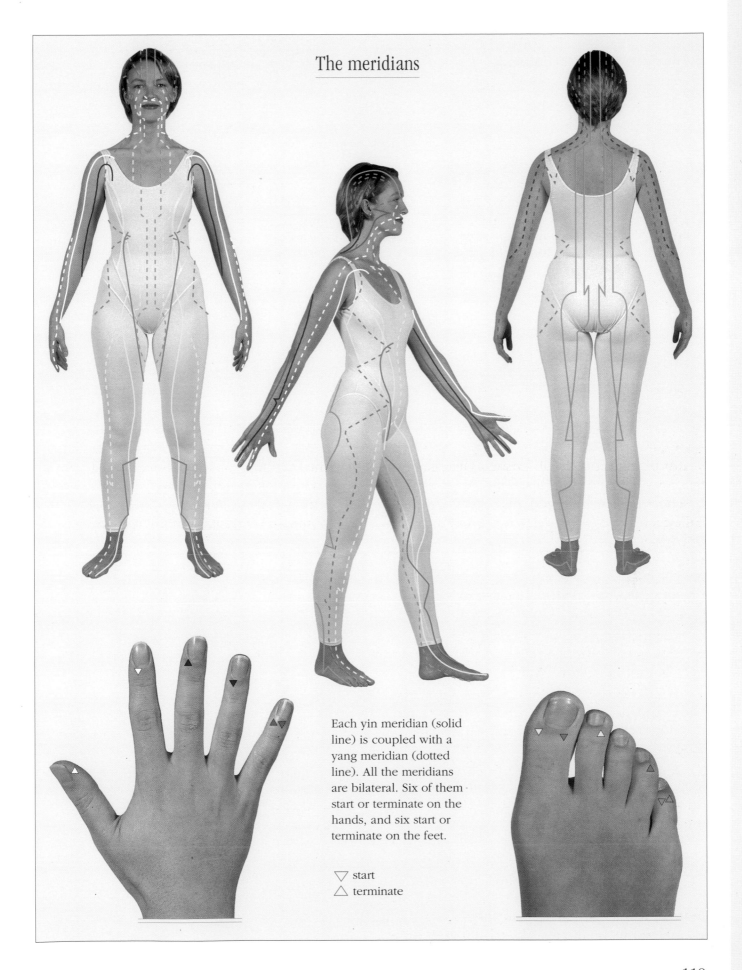

Each yin meridian (solid line) is coupled with a yang meridian (dotted line). All the meridians are bilateral. Six of them start or terminate on the hands, and six start or terminate on the feet.

▽ start
△ terminate

# Elements and attributes associated with meridians

| MERIDIANS | LIVER<br><br>GALL BLADDER | HEART<br><br>SMALL INTESTINE | PERICARDIUM/ CIRCULATION<br><br>TRIPLE HEATER | KIDNEY<br><br>BLADDER | LUNG<br><br>LARGE INTESTINE | SPLEEN/ PANCREAS<br><br>STOMACH |
|---|---|---|---|---|---|---|
| ELEMENT | WOOD | FIRE | FIRE | WATER | METAL | EARTH |
| SEASON | spring | summer | summer | winter | autumn | late summer |
| CLIMATE | wind | heat | heat | cold | dry | dampness humidity |
| ORIFICES | eyes | ears | ears | genitals urethra anus | nose | mouth |
| SENSE ORGAN | eyes | tongue | tongue | ears | nose | mouth |
| BODY PARTS/ TISSUE | muscles sinews | blood vessels | blood vessels | bones bone marrow | skin body hair | flesh body shape |
| FLUID SECRETIONS | tears | perspiration | perspiration | saliva | mucus | saliva |
| SOUND | shouting | laughing | laughing | groaning | crying | singing |
| PHYSICAL MANIFESTATION | nails hands feet | complexion | complexion | head hair | skin body hair | flesh |
| EMOTION | anger | joy happiness | joy happiness | fear | melancholy | sympathy |
| FLAVOUR | sour | bitter | bitter | salty | pungent | sweet |
| COLOUR | green | red | red | blue | white | yellow |

Chinese acupuncture included working with the five elements and their attributes, such as five seasons, five climates, five sounds, five emotions, five colours and various others *(see opposite)*. (The Nei Ching states that each emotion has its seat in an organ. For example, happiness dwells in the heart, sorrow in the lungs, anger in the liver and so on.)

## The meridians and their use in reflexology

Exploring the meridians and the muscles associated with them provides insight into the important role that the meridians play during a reflexology treatment. Reflexology is able to disperse energy blocks and create a state of balance and harmony throughout the whole person. To maintain this state of balance, the cause of the blockage must be dealt with.

If the reflexologist is able to work on the meridians as well as on the reflexes associated with the disharmony in the physical body, a greater sense of wellbeing will be experienced by the patient.

### The liver meridian

The liver meridian is yin and is coupled with the gall bladder meridian which is yang. It has an ascending flow of energy which starts on the back of the big toe and ascends medially up the leg to the genital region. From there, it continues to ascend to just below the nipple on the lower part of the breastbone.

The muscles related to this meridian are the pectoralis major, responsible for specific arm movements, and the rhomboid, which adducts the scapula (shoulder blade) and slightly rotates it downwards.

Malfunction of the liver meridian reflects on the digestive system, producing symptoms such as indigestion, nausea or flatulence. If the liver is over-strained through the intake of alcohol, chocolate, drugs, coffee, tea and so on, headaches and arthritic conditions may occur. The liver affects the eyes and, if in a state of toxicity, may manifest itself in the shape of black dots, or 'floaters', in front of the eyes; cause blurred vision; and produce dry, sore or tired eyes. It is also associated with menstruation, so that malfunction of the liver may exacerbate irregular and painful periods, fluid retention, pre-menstrual tension, poor libido, thrush, uterus and prostate problems. In a male, it can be responsible for a low sperm count.

If this meridian is out of balance, signs of it may appear on a patient's big toe in the form of gout, an ingrowing toenail, and sometimes fungus of the toenail.

### The gall bladder meridian

This meridian is yang and complementary to the liver meridian which is yin. Its pathway runs from the temples, over the head, and down the side of the torso to the back of the fourth toe. The muscles related to it are the deltoid, which abducts, flexes, extends and medially and laterally rotates the arm, and the popliteus, an important muscle which flexes and medially rotates the leg.

The gall bladder stores and secretes the bile produced by the liver. Due to this close connection, any disruptions of the liver will affect it. Malfunction of this meridian can result in headaches, migraine, neck tension, eye problems, painful shoulders, asthma, arthritic hips, knee and menstrual problems.

If the gall bladder meridian is in a state of imbalance, symptoms such as fungus, hammer toe or corns may appear on the fourth toe. Another symptom may be puffiness around the hip reflex.

### The heart meridian

The heart meridian is yin and is coupled with the small intestine which is yang. It has a descending flow of energy which runs from the chest to the hand. A person suffering from angina frequently experiences quite severe pain along this pathway.

The muscle associated with it is the subscapularis, which lies below the scapula and is responsible for rotating the arm medially.

Malfunction of the heart meridian can appear as pain and weakness in the arm or wrist; skin problems; angina; breathlessness and heart attacks. The heart is connected with the tongue, and certain speech defects can be successfully treated by working this meridian. Indications of the meridian's dysfunction could show in nail and finger disorders such as ridges, whitlows, pain and stiffness.

## The small intestine meridian

This meridian is yang and complementary to the heart meridian which is yin. It has an ascending flow of energy which starts on the little finger, runs up the arm, over the shoulder, along the neck to the outer corner of the eye, and terminates just in front of the ear.

The muscles associated with it are the quadriceps, responsible for extending the leg and flexing the thigh, and the abdominal muscles which allow the lateral bend of the spine and compression of the abdomen.

Malfunction of this meridian can cause many kinds of musculo-skeletal pain such as frozen shoulder, stiff neck and tennis elbow. Other disorders include digestive and urinary problems; hearing difficulties, tinnitus and swollen lymph glands in the throat.

Signs on the hands of this meridian's malfunction include arthritis, stiffness in the little finger, and whitlows, white spots, or ridges on the little fingernail.

## Pericardium/circulation meridian

This meridian is yin and is coupled with the triple heater meridian which is yang. It has a descending flow of energy which starts near the nipple and descends down the arm to the back of the middle finger.

The muscles related to it are the gluteus minimus, which abducts and medially rotates the thigh; the adductors, which hold the thigh in and rotate it inwards; the piriformis, which abducts and rotates the thigh laterally, and the gluteus maximus, which extends the hip joint, and extends the trunk when the body rises from a sitting position.

The fibrous body that surrounds and protects the heart is called the pericardium. It contains a lubricant which prevents friction as the heart beats. This is why signs of the malfunction of the pericardium/circulation meridian are very similar to those of the heart meridian, including arthritis, any nail disorder

of the middle finger, and carpal tunnel syndrome (*see page 18*). It is believed that many disorders associated with the heart are treated more effectively on this meridian.

## Triple heater meridian

This meridian is yang and is complementary to the pericardium meridian which is yin. It is not associated with any physical organ, but its function affects the efficiency of the other eleven meridians.

The triple heater meridian has an ascending flow of energy which starts on the back of the ring finger, travels up the arm and ends above the outer corner of the eye.

It comprises three separate 'burners'. The first is located in the chest; the second lies between the diaphragm and the navel; the third is situated in the lower abdomen. When this meridian is functioning correctly, those three areas of the body should be at the same touch-temperature. The main task of the triple heater meridian is to regulate body temperature. If the body is deficient in yin, it will become too hot; and if it is deficient in yang, it will become too cold. As well as regulating body temperature, it balances the autonomic nervous system and controls the pituitary gland – the master gland of the body.

The muscles related to it are the teres minor, or shoulder muscle, responsible for extending and adducting the arm, and rotating it laterally; the sartorius, a thigh muscle which flexes the thigh and rotates it laterally, and also flexes the leg; the gracilis, another thigh muscle, responsible for adducting the thigh and flexing the leg; and the soleus and gastrocnemius, calf muscles which flex the foot as well as the leg.

Disorders associated with this meridian are stiffness and pain along the arm and wrist, plus pain associated with the ear and eye.

Signs on the hands that this meridian is not in balance are arthritis, eczema and nail problems related to the ring finger.

## Kidney meridian

This meridian is yin and is coupled with the bladder meridian which is yang. The kidneys are the foundation for yin and yang: they store the vital essence, jing, which is able to develop into either yin or yang. Consequently, the other organs of the body, which need jing for survival, are dependent upon the bladder. Jing is responsible for the growth and development of a person from the time of conception until death. If there is a lack of jing, then a person could be prone to disease and ill health.

The kidney meridian has an ascending flow of energy. It starts on the sole of the foot and runs up the back of the leg to the front of the body. From there, it ascends in a straight line to the breastbone.

The muscles associated with this meridian are the psoas, which flexes and rotates the thigh laterally and flexes the vertebral column; the upper part of the trapezius, which controls the movements of the shoulder as well as the head; and the iliacus, which flexes and rotates the thigh laterally.

Disorders most often associated with the kidney meridian include brittle and soft bones, back pain, asthma, phlebitis, varicose veins, as well as uterus and prostate problems, and bladder weakness.

Signs on the sole of the foot that indicate problems with this meridian are eczema or fungus on the sole of the foot; painful soles and swollen inner ankles.

### The bladder meridian

The bladder meridian is yang and complementary to the kidney meridian which is yin. This meridian has a descending flow of energy and is one of the longest meridians in the body. It starts at the inner corner of the eye, passes over the head and forks at the base of the neck. One branch runs down along the spine to the coccyx. The other descends to the innermost edge of the scapula and continues down parallel to the first branch. Both branches continue across the buttocks down the back of the leg, joining into one at the back of the knee and ending on the outer edge of the little toe.

The muscles associated with it are the peroneus, which flexes and turns the foot outwards; the sacrospinalis – the largest muscular mass in the back – which is responsible for movements pertaining to the vertebral column and head; the tibialis anterior, which inverts the foot and allows it to bend backwards.

Disorders associated with this meridian include eye weakness, headaches, sinus problems, stiff back, sciatica, knee problems, cystitis and incontinence. Malfunction can be related to problems with the little toe.

### Lung meridian

This meridian is yin and is coupled with the large intestine meridian which is yang. The lungs regulate breathing and may be subjected to conditions such as bronchitis, asthma and emphysema. They also govern the skin. It is well known that people who suffer from eczema and are treated with hydrocortisone cream frequently contract asthma.

The lung meridian has a descending flow of energy which runs from the clavicle, down the arm, ending on the back of the thumb.

The muscles associated with it are the serratus anterior, which rotates the scapula upward and laterally and elevates the ribs when the scapula is fixed; the coracobrachialis, which flexes and adducts the humerus; the deltoids, which abduct, flex, extend and rotate the arm medially and laterally; and the diaphragm. This muscle is a dome-shaped skeletal muscle which lies between the thorax and abdominal cavities, divides the chest from the abdomen, and assists respiration.

Disorders arising from this meridian are infections of the sinuses, throat and chest; asthma; pain in the shoulder or forearm.

On the hands, malfunction of the lung meridian is displayed in problems relating to the thumb. These can occur on the nail, skin or in the joints.

### Large intestine meridian

This meridian is yang and complementary to the lung meridian which is yin. The large intestine is responsible for the elimination of waste material from the body. If this organ is not functioning correctly, it can cause a build up of toxins in the body. Due to their close link, either of these two meridians not working efficiently will affect the other.

The large intestine meridian has an ascending flow of energy which starts at the back of the index finger, runs up the arm and neck and ends below the nose.

The muscles associated with it are the tensor fasciae latae, which flexes and abducts the thigh; the hamstrings, responsible for flexing the leg and extending the thigh; and the quadratus lumborum, which aids in the lateral bend of the spine.

Malfunction of the large intestine meridian can lead to nose and throat problems, a greasy or spotty skin, frozen shoulder, tennis elbow and bursitis.

On the hands, any disorder connected to this meridian will manifest itself in the index finger. It could include problems with the nail or arthritic joints.

## Spleen/pancreas meridian

This meridian is yin and is coupled with the stomach meridian which is yang. The spleen encompasses a wide range of functions. It is closely linked to the stomach, assisting in the transformation of food and drink into ch'i – or energy – and blood.

The spleen/pancreas meridian has an ascending flow of energy which starts in the centre of the back of the big toe, runs up the leg, through the body, and ends on the side of the breast, under the armpit.

The muscles related to this meridian are the latissimus dorsi, which extends, adducts and rotates the arm medially and also draws the arm downward and backward; the trapezius, which is responsible for the movement of the scapula; the extensor pollicis longus, which extends the thumb and abducts the wrist; and finally the triceps, which is responsible for extending the arm.

The main disorders associated with this meridian are fatigue, digestive problems, diarrhoea and metabolic problems. Because it starts on the big toe, problems related to the big toe can be indicative that this meridian is not functioning correctly.

## Stomach meridian

This meridian is yang and complementary to the spleen/pancreas meridian which is yin. The stomach is the organ of the body where food and drink are broken down, in preparation for the absorption of vital nutrients into the body. The spleen/pancreas is responsible for helping this process, therefore the two meridians work closely together.

The stomach meridian has a descending flow of energy. It starts beneath the eye and moves up to the temple before continuing down the body to the top of the second toe.

The muscles related to this meridian are the pectoralis major, which adducts and rotates the arm medially; the levator scapulae, which elevates the scapula and slightly rotates it downwards; the neck muscles, and the brachioradialis, which flexes the elbow and helps turn the wrist.

Disharmony of this meridian can lead to problems associated with the stomach, eyes, sinuses, throat, spleen and pancreas. These are mirrored on the second toe in the form of corns, fungus of the nail and malformation of the bones.

---

### A word of advice

When working with meridians during a reflexology treatment, begin on the points on the toes or fingers where the meridians terminate or start. It is advisable to use the pressure-point technique, also known as the pivoting movement.

Colour, which is explained in the next section, can also be used on these points.

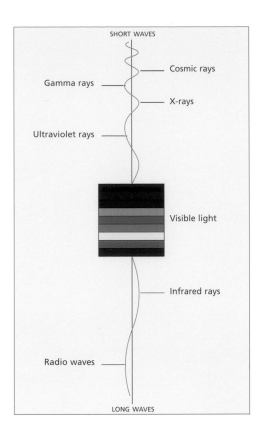

Above *The electromagnetic spectrum.*

# Treating with colour and reflexology

Colour is a phenomenon which surrounds us and which is often taken for granted. It is displayed in full glory through the wonder of the rainbow and the awe-inspiring spectacle of the polar lights, known as the aurora borealis. Colours are the visible part of what is known as the electromagnetic spectrum.

This spectrum comprises different kinds of energy waves which range from radio waves – the longest – to cosmic energy waves – the shortest. Between these are found infrared rays, visible light (which embodies the colours of the spectrum), ultraviolet rays, X-rays and gamma rays.

Electromagnetic energy travels at approximately 300,000 kilometres (186,000 miles) per second. It is used by science in the form of radio waves and infrared rays, and by medicine in the form of X-rays and gamma rays. The latter can be detrimental to health. What I fail to comprehend is why scientists and

doctors refute the effect that visible light can have on a human being while acknowledging the effect of invisible energy waves. If the other energy waves of the electromagnetic spectrum affect us, why not colour?

The rediscovery of colour used as a therapy is still in its infancy. Historical research shows that it was practised in many cultures. The Atlanteans (inhabitants of the vanished continent Atlantis) are believed to have built healing temples whose domed ceilings were made of interlocking crystals that dissipated the light into the colour spectrum. These colours were used to treat disease, childbirth, heal relationships and assist the soul in its transition from this life to the next.

Archaeologists have discovered that the Egyptians had individual healing rooms in their temples built in such a way that each

# Treatment colours and their complementary colours

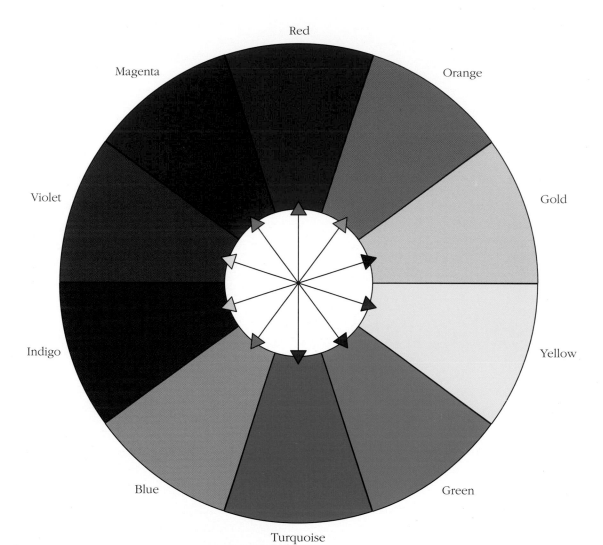

Red

Magenta

Orange

Violet

Gold

Indigo

Yellow

Blue

Green

Turquoise

## The red spectrum

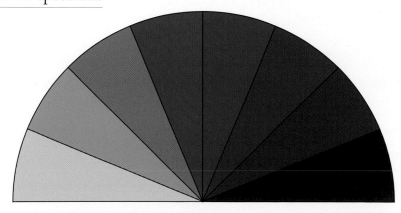

All the treatment colours hold a complementary colour – always used with the treatment colour in therapy – indicated by arrows in the colour wheel (*above*).

Every colour also also has its own spectrum which ranges from very deep to very pale, as shown here on the red spectrum (*left*).

one attracted individual rays of the spectrum. It is generally believed that those who came to the temple for healing were first 'colour diagnosed' and then placed in the room where the prescribed colour radiated.

India, a country alive with colour, still uses colour in gem therapy. Indian gem therapists believe that gems are the storehouses of cosmic colour, and that everything manifest is composed of the seven rays which are the primeval, formative forces of nature. This means that a person suffering from some form of disease should be treated with the relevant colour or colours.

Our ancestors, aware of how the colours of nature affected them, knew how to absorb and use these for healing. Unlike us, who spend a great deal of time indoors and are more often than not subjected to the detrimental effects of artificial light, they spent most of their time outdoors, surrounded by the wonderful array of colour that nature offers. Anthropologists believe that colour vision was not yet developed in pre-historic man, and came at a later stage of evolution. Even if this were true, the colour rays would still have had a marked effect upon him.

At the beginning of the nineteenth century, colour therapy was temporarily replaced by allopathic medicine due to the discovery of new drugs and advances in surgery. It is interesting to note that some of the early pioneers of allopathic medicine used colour in their treatments. One of the most famous of these was Hippocrates (460-370 BC), a Greek physician regarded as the father of medicine and originator of the Hippocratic oath.

Colour is derived from light; but in order to produce colour, there has to be an inter-action between darkness and light. One way of experiencing this phenomenon is to shine light through a prism. The prism refracts the light, splitting it into the multicoloured band known as the colour spectrum. The reason the spectrum can be seen is because each of the colours has its own angle of refraction.

The colours produced from the refraction of light are red, orange, yellow, green, turquoise, blue, indigo, violet and magenta.

Each of these colours has its own wavelength and sound frequency. These range from the longest wavelength and lowest sound frequency of red, to the shortest wavelength and highest sound frequency of magenta.

All the colours of the spectrum hold a complementary colour – always used with the treatment colour in therapy – and possess their own specific therapeutic properties, which are given below.

### Red – complementary colour turquoise

Red is a primary colour, which means that it cannot be produced by mixing any other colours. It is the colour with the longest wavelength and lowest sound frequency. Like all the other colours, it has its own spectrum which ranges from a very deep to a very pale red. It is a powerful energizer and stimulant; and it is aligned to the masculine energy. If it is used in excess, it can cause aggression and sometimes restlessness.

Red is the symbol of life, strength and vitality and helps to ground us. Red is the dominant colour of the base chakra and is connected to the gonads and reproductive cycle. This makes it a good colour to use in cases of infertility. It works with the haemoglobin to increase energy, raise body temperature and improve circulation and is therefore beneficial in cases of low blood pressure, anaemia and iron deficieny. When it is used with its complementary colour turquoise, red can help counteract infections and pneumonia, and alleviate constipation.

When red is mixed with white, it produces rose pink, the colour of spiritual love. Rose pink can be used in conjunction with violet for a broken heart. Violet restores dignity and self-respect and rose pink fills the person with spiritual love.

In therapy, red should not be used when there is anxiety, emotional distress, high blood pressure or asthma.

### Orange – complementary colour blue

Orange is a combination of red and yellow, thereby influencing both physical vitality and the intellect (*see* Yellow *below*). Related to the adrenal glands, it is the dominant colour of the sacral chakra and is symbolic of the feminine energy of creation.

This is the colour of joy, the colour of dance, and as such is good for treating depression. Its antispasmodic effect works in cases of muscle spasms and cramp. It is also used in cases of kidney stones, stones in the gall bladder, or for colds, underactive thyroid and bronchitis.

Orange is associated with the splenic chakra through which prana – etheric energy – is absorbed. This makes it a good colour for treating fatigue or exhaustion.

### Gold - complementary colour indigo
Gold is the colour of wisdom and is indicative of high spirituality. In healing, this colour is only used with its complementary colour indigo, and for energizing the body at the end of treatment.

### Yellow - complementary colour violet
Yellow is one of the three primary pigment colours. Like the other two, red and blue, it cannot be produced by mixing any other colours. Yellow is related to the solar plexus chakra which governs the pancreas, controls the digestive system and helps to purify the body through its eliminating action on both the liver and the intestines.

The yellow rays carry positive, magnetic currents which are inspiring and stimulating. These rays strengthen the nerves, stimulate the intellect and activate the motor nerves in the physical body, thereby generating energy in the muscles. This colour is used to treat partial or complete paralysis, diabetes, indigestion, fractured or broken bones and all arthritic conditions.

Yellow works on the skin by improving its texture, cleansing, healing scars, and helping conditions such as eczema and psoriasis.

### Green - complementary colour magenta
This colour is a combination of yellow and blue. Yellow being the last colour on the magnetic side of the spectrum and blue, the first on the electrical side, green is the colour of balance. It is the dominant colour of the heart chakra and has the power to harmonize the yin and yang – the positive and negative energies of the body. It also has a harmonizing effect on the three aspects of a human being, namely body, mind and spirit.

When green is administered through the throat chakra, it cleanses the etheric body – that part of the aura nearest to the physical body – where disease is first manifest.

Green possesses antiseptic properties, enabling it to be used in cases of infection. It also has the ability to detoxify, which makes it invaluable for use on a toxic liver. Other disorders for which green is helpful are constipation, shock and certain heart conditions.

Dr William Kelly, an American doctor, working with green light, found that in certain circumstances it destroyed embryonic cell structure. In view of this, it is advisable to apply green light only to the heart chakra in the case of pregnant women.

### Turquoise - complementary colour red
Turquoise is a combination of blue and green. It is not connected with one of the seven major chakras, but with a minor one related to the thymus gland and located close to it. The thymus gland is part of our immune system, therefore turquoise is a good colour to use to strengthen this. It can also be helpful in prolonging the life of AIDS sufferers, since the immune system is attacked by the AIDS virus.

Turquoise has the ability to calm, making it an excellent colour to use for nervous tension. When applied with its complementary colour red, it helps to combat infection.

### Blue - complementary colour orange
Blue is the dominant colour of the throat chakra. Like red, it is a primary or pure colour. But unlike red, which acts as a stimulant, blue has a relaxing and expanding effect, and is used on asthmatics.

Because it is symbolic of tranquillity, peace, inspiration and devotion, blue is an excellent colour for healing and for meditation. Moreover, it is an efficient colour to wear during the period of pregnancy.

The throat represents the bridge that must be crossed in order to move from the physical to the spiritual realm. It is also the centre of communication and creativity. Those people who communicate with difficulty, or work mainly with their intellect, will benefit from treatment with the blue ray. Other disorders which respond well to blue are tension, fear, insomnia, anxiety, jaundice, diarrhoea, and mastitis (inflammation of the breast).

When blue is administered with its complementary colour orange, it brings about a state of peaceful joy. However, an excess of blue light can cause depression.

### Indigo – complementary colour gold

This colour is a combination of blue and violet and is related to the brow chakra. It is associated with the mind, eyes and ears, and therefore it is used for cataracts and sinus problems. Being so closely related to the blue ray, it can help with conditions relating to the throat. Indigo is a strong painkiller and has antiseptic properties.

Indigo, applied with its complementary colour gold, is used for headaches, neuralgic pain, insomnia, eye strain, angina, muscular strains, hepatitis, inflammation and sciatica.

### Violet – complementary colour yellow

This colour is related to the crown chakra and pertains to spirituality, self-respect and dignity. Violet can lead us into the realm of spiritual awareness, where it becomes the last gateway we must pass through in order to become united with our true self – or inner divine being. It is also related to insight and inspiration.

Violet is very beneficial to psychological disorders such as schizophrenia and manic depression. It also helps sciatica, diseases of the scalp and all disorders connected with the nervous system.

### Magenta – complementary colour green

Magenta is composed of red and violet and is associated with release or 'letting go'. On a mental level, magenta enables us to let go of ideas and thought patterns which have become irrelevant. Emotionally, it helps us to let go of old feelings which are preventing us from moving forward. On the physical level, it leads us to relinquish physical activities which we have outgrown.

Magenta, with its complementary colour green, can help with the treatment of cancer. Any work with infectious, life-threatening, or terminal diseases, however, should always be carried out in conjunction with the medical profession. Magenta is also beneficial in cases of tinnitus, benign cysts and detached retinas.

## Treatment with colour

A table showing the correct colours to use for treatment is given on the following pages. It includes the general reflex colour, and the treatment colour – with its complementary colour – to use for some of the more common complaints associated with a reflex.

Left *A polyhedron, or glass prism. It is able to refract white light that passes through it, splitting it into the colours of the spectrum.*

# Reflex and complaints treatment colours

The general reflex colour, always followed by its complementary colour, is used when treating a painful reflex that is not associated with a specific complaint.

When you treat a specific complaint, use the main treatment colour related to the complaint, and always follow it with its complementary colour, which acts as a fixative.

The average length of time that a colour should be administered is 30 seconds for the treatment colour, and 30 seconds for the complementary colour. This can differ with individual patients, so learn to listen and follow your intuition.

| Reflex | General reflex colour | Complaint | Colours for specific complaints | |
|--------|----------|-----------|----------------|------------------|
| | | | treatment colour | complementary colour |
| Spine | | Paralysis | | |
| | | Spinal meningitis | | |
| | | Pain | | |
| Head | | Epilepsy | | |
| | | Headaches, neuralgic pain | | |
| | | Insomnia | | |
| | | Head colds | | |
| | | Scalp complaints | | |
| Pituitary | | Tumours | | |
| Sinuses | | Sinusitis, colds and catarrh | | |
| | | Constipation | | |
| | | Pain | | |
| Neck | | Stiff neck | | |
| | | Sore throat | | |
| Eyes | | Eye strain | | |
| | | Cataracts | | |
| | | Detached retina | | |
| | | Glaucoma | | |
| Ears | | Tinnitus | | |
| | | Ear infections | | |
| Thyroid | | Goitre | | |
| | | Over active | | |
| | | Under active | | |
| Parathyroids | | Osteoporosis | | |
| Lungs | | Asthma | | |
| | | Bronchitis | | |
| | | Pleurisy | | |
| | | Cancer | | |
| | | Pneumonia | | |
| Heart | | Tachycardia | | |
| | | Palpitations | | |
| | | Thrombosis | | |
| | | Angina | | |
| | | Broken heart (emotional) | | |
| Shoulder | | Frozen shoulder | | |
| | | Muscular strains or tension | | |

| Reflex | General reflex colour | Complaint | Colours for specific complaints | |
|---|---|---|---|---|
| | | | treatment colour | complementary colour |
| Solar plexus | | Tension, stress | | |
| Gall bladder | | Stones | | |
| Liver | | Hepatitis | | |
| | | Jaundice | | |
| Stomach | | Indigestion | | |
| | | Ulcers | | |
| | | Cancer | | |
| Pancreas | | Diabetes | | |
| Kidneys | | Nephritis | | |
| | | Kidney stones | | |
| | | Nephroma | | |
| | | Water retention | | |
| Bladder | | Cystitis | | |
| Small intestine | | Inflammation | | |
| | | Cancer | | |
| Ileo-caecal valve | | Constipation | | |
| Colon | | Constipation | | |
| | | Diarrhoea | | |
| | | Cancer | | |
| Sciatic loop | | Sciatica | | |
| Spleen | | General treatment | | |
| Ovaries | | Ovarian cyst | | |
| | | Pregnancy | | |
| | | Infertility | | |
| Uterus | | Prolapse | | |
| | | Pregnancy | | |
| | | Tumour | | |
| | | Fibroids | | |
| | | Infertility | | |
| Breast | | Cysts | | |
| | | Cancer | | |
| | | Mastitis | | |
| Lymphatic system | | General treatment | | |
| Sacro-iliac joint | | Arthritis | | |
| Prostate | | Enlarged | | |
| Testes | | Malignant tumour | | |
| Anus | | Piles | | |

## Key to colours

- RED
- ORANGE
- GOLD
- YELLOW
- GREEN
- TURQUOISE
- BLUE
- INDIGO
- VIOLET
- MAGENTA
- ROSE PINK

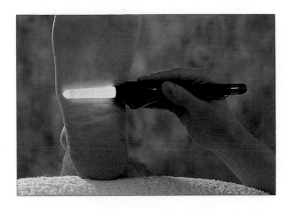

# How to use colour with reflexology

When using colour with reflexology, a normal reflexology treatment is carried out first. This acts as a diagnostic tool, in addition to working with energy blocks in the body. After completing the treatment, colour is administered – together with its complementary colour – to the zones which were found to be painful, as well as to the zones related to the patient's complaint. The colour treatment ends by stabilizing the chakras situated along the spinal reflex of the feet or the hands. It is followed by channelling gold – the golden light of the universe – through the soles of your patient's feet. The effect of gold light is to re-energize the body.

The most beautiful instrument we can use to administer colour is our own physical body. After visualizing the required colour, we allow it to be channelled through our hands and fingers into the relevant part of the feet or hands of our patient.

In order to be able to do this, we must learn to visualize colour, to sensitize our body to its vibrational frequency and turn it into a clear channel for the transmission of colour. This involves time and self-discipline. But having to face new challenges enables us to grow in strength and understanding, and we may become better equipped to help others.

For reflexologists who find the task of sensitizing the physical body too demanding a challenge, the reflexology torch has been devised. This torch possesses a special head into which is fixed a quartz crystal. A stained glass disc – of the appropriate colour – is inserted into the head, and when the torch is switched on, the light filters through and floods the quartz crystal with the required colour. This is then administered, followed by its complementary colour, for twenty to thirty seconds on the relevant reflex or reflexes.

Stained glass is preferable to gels for the filters, because it contains the complete spectrum of the colour it displays, unlike gels which only exhibit one frequency of any colour. For a patient who does not require that frequency, the treatment is less beneficial.

It is best to use the torch in a darkened room, so as to prevent the dilution of colour by daylight. I have found that, apart from the torch being a powerful instrument, patients love to see the colour. And depending upon their sensitivity, some patients are able to *feel* the colour pulsating through their body.

From the first moment that I was privileged to work with, and later to teach the use of colour with reflexology, some wonderful results were obtained – both by me and my students. I know that there is still a great deal to learn about the combination of these two therapies. But I know, too, that many people have been helped physically, mentally and spiritually by the use of colour.

Above *Reflexology colour torch, shown here treating the transverse colon reflex.*

# Reflex colours on the feet and hands

This and the following charts are designed to give the general colour used for the reflexes on both the feet and the hands. A difference in the shade of a colour is deliberate, and intended merely to make it easier to identify two reflexes of the same colour.

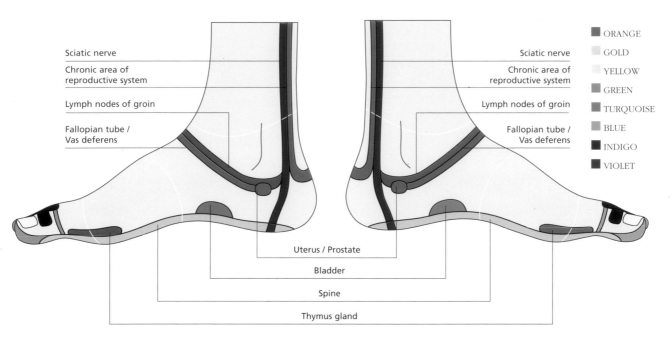

Sciatic nerve
Chronic area of reproductive system
Lymph nodes of groin
Fallopian tube / Vas deferens

Sciatic nerve
Chronic area of reproductive system
Lymph nodes of groin
Fallopian tube / Vas deferens

- ORANGE
- GOLD
- YELLOW
- GREEN
- TURQUOISE
- BLUE
- INDIGO
- VIOLET

Uterus / Prostate

Bladder

Spine

Thymus gland

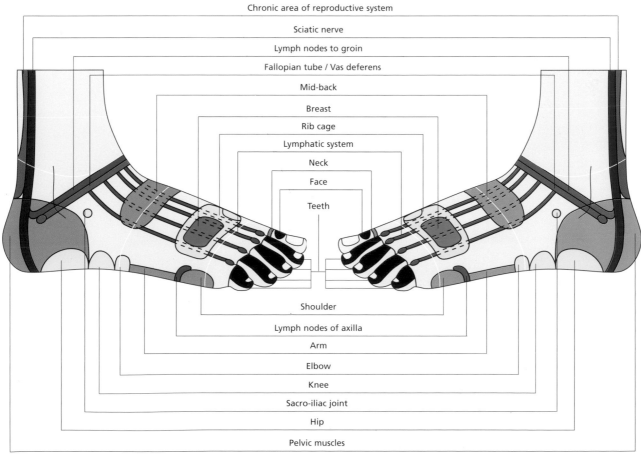

Chronic area of reproductive system

Sciatic nerve

Lymph nodes to groin

Fallopian tube / Vas deferens

Mid-back

Breast

Rib cage

Lymphatic system

Neck

Face

Teeth

Shoulder

Lymph nodes of axilla

Arm

Elbow

Knee

Sacro-iliac joint

Hip

Pelvic muscles

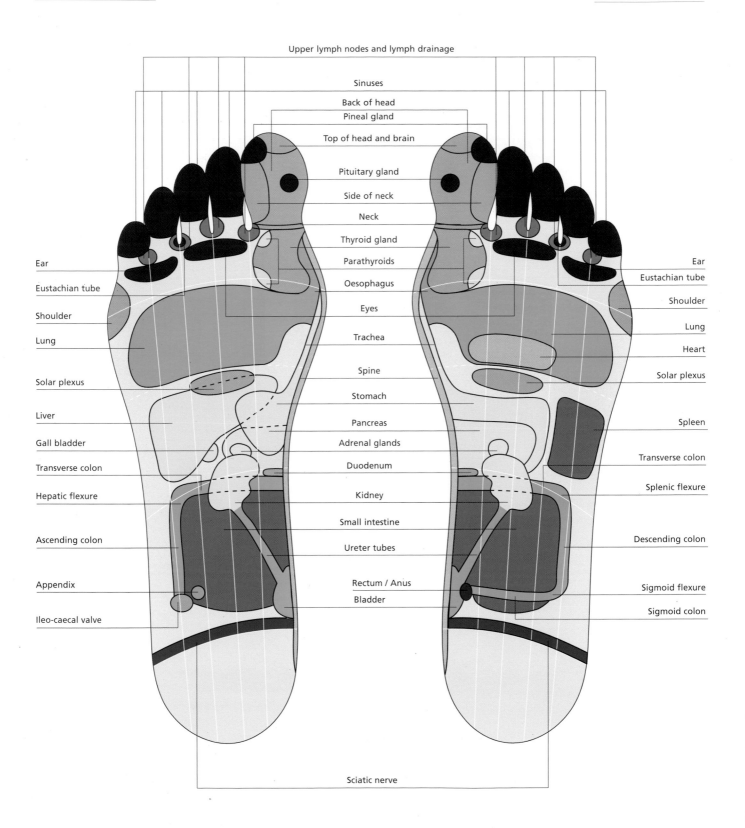

Upper lymph nodes and lymph drainage

Sinuses

Back of head

Pineal gland

Top of head and brain

Pituitary gland

Side of neck

Neck

Thyroid gland

Parathyroids

Oesophagus

Eyes

Trachea

Spine

Stomach

Pancreas

Adrenal glands

Duodenum

Kidney

Small intestine

Ureter tubes

Rectum / Anus

Bladder

Ear

Eustachian tube

Shoulder

Lung

Solar plexus

Liver

Gall bladder

Transverse colon

Hepatic flexure

Ascending colon

Appendix

Ileo-caecal valve

Ear

Eustachian tube

Shoulder

Lung

Heart

Solar plexus

Spleen

Transverse colon

Splenic flexure

Descending colon

Sigmoid flexure

Sigmoid colon

Sciatic nerve

# Top of left foot

# Top of right foot

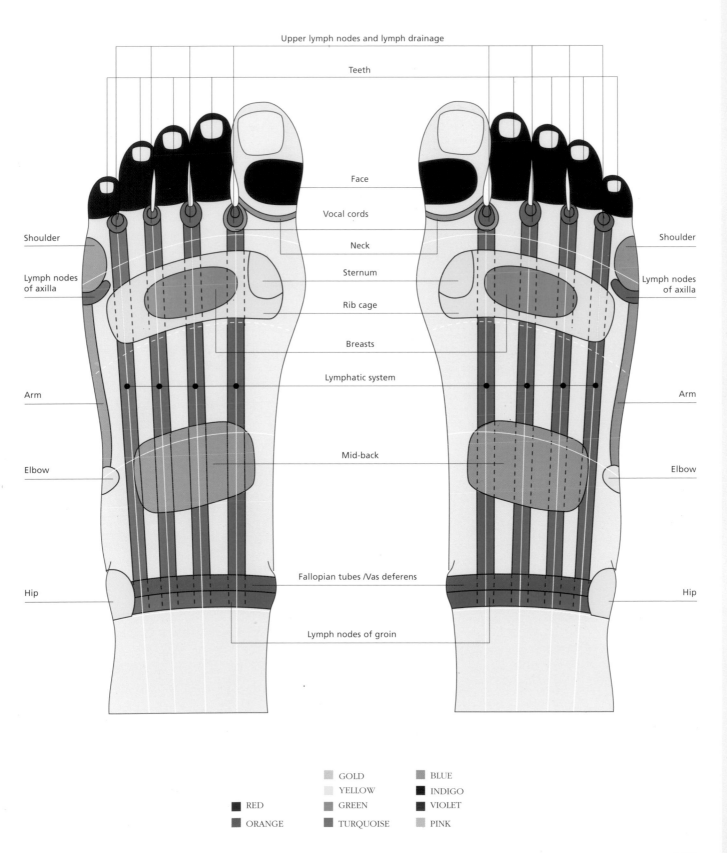

Upper lymph nodes and lymph drainage

Teeth

Face

Vocal cords

Shoulder

Neck

Lymph nodes
of axilla

Sternum

Rib cage

Breasts

Lymphatic system

Arm

Mid-back

Elbow

Fallopian tubes /Vas deferens

Hip

Lymph nodes of groin

Shoulder

Lymph nodes
of axilla

Arm

Elbow

Hip

- GOLD
- YELLOW
- GREEN
- TURQUOISE
- BLUE
- INDIGO
- VIOLET
- PINK
- RED
- ORANGE

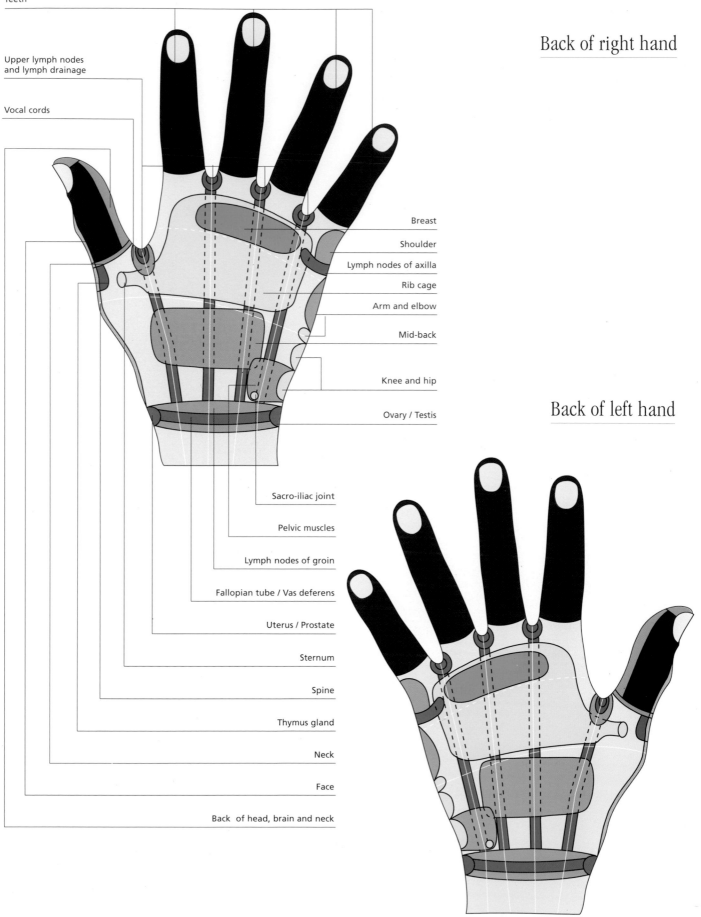

Teeth

Upper lymph nodes
and lymph drainage

Vocal cords

Breast

Shoulder

Lymph nodes of axilla

Rib cage

Arm and elbow

Mid-back

Knee and hip

Ovary / Testis

Back of left hand

Sacro-iliac joint

Pelvic muscles

Lymph nodes of groin

Fallopian tube / Vas deferens

Uterus / Prostate

Sternum

Spine

Thymus gland

Neck

Face

Back of head, brain and neck

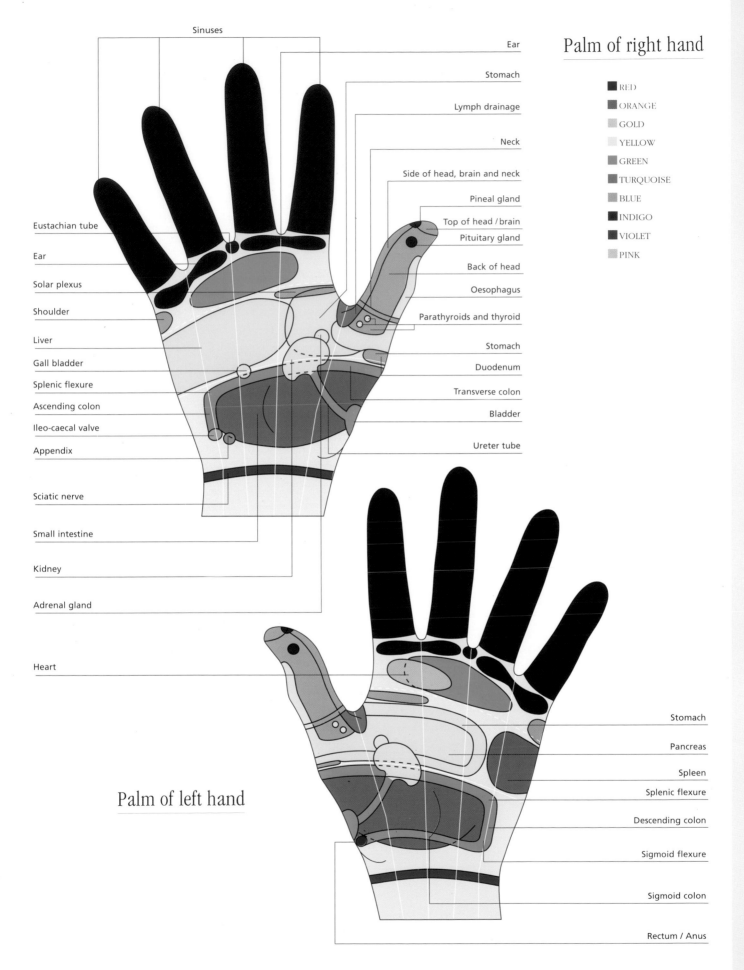

Sinuses

Ear

Stomach

Lymph drainage

Neck

Side of head, brain and neck

Pineal gland

Top of head / brain

Pituitary gland

Back of head

Oesophagus

Parathyroids and thyroid

Stomach

Duodenum

Transverse colon

Bladder

Ureter tube

Eustachian tube

Ear

Solar plexus

Shoulder

Liver

Gall bladder

Splenic flexure

Ascending colon

Ileo-caecal valve

Appendix

Sciatic nerve

Small intestine

Kidney

Adrenal gland

Heart

## Palm of right hand

- ■ RED
- ■ ORANGE
- ■ GOLD
- ■ YELLOW
- ■ GREEN
- ■ TURQUOISE
- ■ BLUE
- ■ INDIGO
- ■ VIOLET
- ■ PINK

## Palm of left hand

Stomach

Pancreas

Spleen

Splenic flexure

Descending colon

Sigmoid flexure

Sigmoid colon

Rectum / Anus

# Self-help

When enlisting the help of reflexology with a health problem, it is always advisable to seek treatment by a qualified practitioner. However, if this proves difficult, then self-help can be attempted.

If you decide to treat yourself, first read through the cautions given in Part One. Use reflexology on your hands, because they are more accessible than your feet and therefore easier to treat.

Always give yourself a complete treatment, rather than treating only the reflexes related to any particular disorders. When you come to the end of the treatment, return to any reflexes that you have found to be painful.

Be careful not to overstimulate the body. Remember that reflexology activates it to heal itself, and that part of this process is the elimination of toxins. For this reason, treatment carried out too frequently, or a prolonged treatment, could make you feel quite ill in the days that follow. I recommend that you give yourself no more than two treatments in any one week. If you work carefully and methodically, you should experience a general improvement in your health.

# Patient advice

If you have decided to seek reflexology treatment from a practitioner, make sure that the person you choose holds a certificate of qualification from a recognized reflexology school. When making an appointment, ask the reflexologist where he or she studied. Then contact the school indicated in order to make sure that the person's name appears on their register of practitioners.

In Britain, a further check can be made through the Institute for Complementary Medicine (I.C.M.) *(see page 141)*. The I.C.M. is able to give information on the schools that are recognized as teaching to the required standard. It will also give names of practitioners that are on the British Register of Complementary Practitioners. In order to be entered in this register, a practitioner must hold a qualification from a recognized school, and to have been in practise for three or more years.

The recommended number of treatments is normally a minimum of six. Follow the advice given, even if this initially proves to be difficult. Remember that, ultimately, you are responsible for your own health and therefore responsible for what you do to your body. If you are able to work with the reflexologist, I am confident that, in time, you will experience an improvement in health, a greater sense of well-being and an increase in energy.

# Conclusion

As well as being a mirror image of the human body, the feet and hands play a further role through the medium of toes and fingers. Unfortunately, through our loss of sensitivity and our unnatural way of living, this role has been largely lost.

The big or first toe is known as the flusher, because it has the capacity to flush negativity out of the system. The second toe is called the wayfinder; it enables the meridian and organ associated with it, namely the stomach, to sense direction, and the way to bring things to fruition. The third toe is able to detect animal magnetism, especially in relation to the opposite sex. The fourth toe is used as a monitor of temperature: it compares the body temperature with the temperature outside. On the fifth toe resides a receptor formed by the kidney and bladder meridians; given the right conditions, this receptor is able to tell our intuition which medicinal foods we need.

On the hand, the thumb is associated with integrity. The more a thumb curves and points away from the body, the less integrity a person has. The index finger is the finger of guilt and shame, the finger that points out right and wrong. The middle finger is the most receptive. It extends the furthest, and therefore contacts energies before any of the other fingers. The ring finger is the finger of integration and grounding. The little finger is the finger of prosperity. For those who believe in reincarnation, this finger also reflects absence of prosperity in previous lives, with starvation, poverty and homelessness.

If our hands and feet were indeed sensitive to such knowledge at one stage of our evolution, practising a holistic therapy such as reflexology can help us regain this sensitivity. Reflexology requires us to sentisize our body to nature and the vibrations that surround us. But it takes time, discipline and dedication. Learn to tune in to nature. Walk barefoot in the garden or the countryside. Learn to feel the vibrational frequencies of stones, plants, crystals and colours through your hands and feet. Learn to listen to your inner voice or intuition. When you work, try and wear only clothes made of natural fibers, such as cotton or silk: manmade fibres restrict the electromagnetic field that surrounds us and thereby inhibit our connecting with nature.

In concluding this book, I would like to share some of the ideas that were put forward by Hanne Marquardt, author of *Reflex Zone Therapy of the Feet,* at a recent conference which I attended.

Feet, which are the object of reflexology, are something which all people possess, in all nations and all walks of life. Feet must be regarded as a common factor of unity. When reflexologists give a treatment, they do so with bowed head – a sign of humility derived from the knowledge that the ability to help a fellow being is a privilege.

Patients usually come to be treated for a particular disease. But could not disease also be written as 'dis-ease', not being at ease with life? Reflexologists, as therapists, do not treat diseases. We treat people. We treat the patient as a whole person, which means that we treat the sum total of everything. The plantar aspect of the foot is the sole – a reminder that in treating the sum total of everything, the soul must be included. In helping patients to restore their health, the therapist is helping them to cope with the stimulus encountered through living.

I believe that pure, unconditional love is also a remedy against disease. If we as therapists are able to project this onto our patients and teach them to love themselves, the healing process is accelerated. The feet are a microcosm of the whole body. In the same way, we too are a microcosm – within the macrocosm of cosmic, healing love.

# Glossary

**Anaemia** a deficiency in the number of red blood cells in the blood, or in haemoglobin, leading to tiredness, pallor and shortness of breath.

**Angina** the name given to pain arising when the muscular wall of the heart becomes temporarily short of oxygen by failure of the coronary arteries.

**Autonomic nervous system** part of the nervous system, consisting of visceral nerve cells that transmit impulses from the central nervous system to smooth muscles, cardiac muscles and glands.

**Axilla** the technical name for armpit.

**Bilirubin** orange-yellow bile pigment produced from the breakdown of haemoglobin. It gives the faeces their brown colour.

**Bursa** a sac interposed between opposing surfaces that slide past each other. The bursa contains lubricating fluid which permits free motion.

**Bursitis** inflammation of the bursa which causes pain in the joints.

**Candida albicans** a fungus that commonly affects the mouth, intestinal tract or vagina. It tends to grow in moist areas of the body, but it can cause painful inflammation round the nails of people whose hands are often in water. In certain circumstances, the fungus can grow rapidly, causing the illness known as thrush.

**Cerebellum** a division of the brain concerned with the balance of the body and the orderly performance of muscular activity.

**Chronic area of reproductive system** the reflex area related to any chronic or long lasting disease of the reproductive system.

**Clavicle** the technical name for the collarbone which links the shoulder blade to the breastbone.

**Coronary artery** either of the two arteries which supply blood to the muscles of the heart.

**Endocrine system** this is composed of the endocrine glands, specialized organs in the body which secrete chemical substances, called hormones, directly into the blood stream. They play an important part in general chemical changes in the body and particular activities of other organs.

**Endometriosis** the presence of endometrium in areas other than the lining of the uterus, which produces pain.

**Endometrium** the inner mucous membrane which lines the uterus.

**Haemoglobin** a substance which carries oxygen in the red blood cells and gives blood its red colour.

**Hepatitis** a viral infection which affects the liver cells, often leading to severe liver damage.

**Ileum** the terminal portion of the small intestine which leads into the large intestine.

**Immune system** the various defence mechanisms produced by the body in response to most types of infection. The thymus gland plays an important part in stimulating some of these mechanisms.

**Infrared rays** electromagnetic radiation occupying part of the electromagnetic spectrum. Infrared radiation has a lower frequency than visible red light. It is normally produced by heat.

**Jaundice** a yellow colour of the skin, whites of the eyes and other tissues. Jaundice is not a disease. It occurs whenever the concentration of bile pigment in the blood is increased – whatever the reason.

**Lateral** in reflexology, the side of the foot, hand, fingers or toes which faces away from the body; also called the external side.

**Libido** a psychoanalytical term to describe a form of psychic energy emanating from the unconscious; principally, a sexual urge.

**Medial** in reflexology, the side of the foot, hand, fingers or toes which faces towards the body; also called the inner side.

**Melatonin** the hormone secreted by the pineal gland, believed to be involved in the reproductive function.

**Ridges** any elongated, raised borders on a bone, tooth, nail and so on.

**Thrush** see candida albicans.

**Varicose veins** swollen, distended veins which can be seen through the skin and may lead to congestion of the circulation, or even burst and bleed.

# Further reading

Artley, Malvin N., Jr. *Bodies of Fire*. Vol. 1. Jersey City Heights, NJ, USA: University of the Seven Rays Publishing House, 1992.

Brennan, Barbara Ann. *Hands of Light*. New York, USA: Bantam Books, 1988.
——. *Light Emerging*. New York, USA: Bantam Books, 1993.

Carper, Jean. *Food Your Miracle Medicine*. London: Simon & Schuster Ltd, 1993.

Dethlefsen, Thorwald, and Dahlke Rüdiger. *The Healing Power of Illness,* translated by Peter Lemesurier. Shaftesbury: Element Books Ltd, 1990.

Dougans, Inge, with Suzanne Ellis. *The Art of Reflexology*. Shaftesbury: Element Books Ltd, 1992.

Gimbel, Theo. *The Book of Colour Healing*. London: Gaia Books Ltd, 1994.

Grinberg, Avi. *Holistic Reflexology*. Wellingborough, Northants: Thorsons Publishers Ltd, 1989.

——. *Foot Analysis – The Footpath to Self Discovery*. York Beach, ME, USA: Samuel Weiser Inc., 1993.

Hall, Nicola M. *Reflexology – A Way to Better Health*. Bath: Gateway Books, 1991.
——. *Reflexology for Women*. London: Thorsons Publishers Ltd, 1994.

Ingham, Eunice. *Stories the Feet Can Tell*. St Petersburgh, Florida: Ingham Publishing Inc., 1938.
——. *Stories the Feet Have Told*. New York, USA: Bantam Books, 1951.

Norman, Laura. *The Reflexology Handbook*. London: Judy Piatkus, 1989.

Shapiro, Debbie. *The Bodymind Workbook*. Shaftesbury: Element Books Ltd, 1990.

Wills, Pauline. *The Reflexology and Colour Therapy Workbook*. Shaftesbury: Element Books Ltd, 1992.
——. *Colour Therapy*. Shaftesbury: Element Books Ltd, 1993.
——. *Visualisation*. London: Hodder & Stoughton, 1994.

## Useful addresses

**United Kingdom**
The Bayly School of
Reflexology
Monks Orchard
Whitbourne
Worcester WR6 5RB
Telephone 01886 821207

Chrysalis School of Reflexology
14 Central Avenue
Cookstown
Co. Tyrone BT80 8AT
N. Ireland
Telephone 06487 63664

Colour and Reflexology
9 Wyndale Avenue
Kingsbury
London NW9 9PT
Telephone 0181 204 7672

Institute of Complementary
Medicine (I.C.M.)
Tavern Quay
Plough Way
Surrey Quays
London SE16 1QZ
Telephone 0171 237 5165

International Association
for Colour Therapy
137 Hendon Lane
Finchley
London N3 3PR
Telephone 0181 349 3299

**Australia**
Reflexology Association of
Australia
22 Lagoon St
(PO Box 841)
Narrabeen NSW 2101
Telephone 02 970 6155

# Index

# Acknowledgements

The author wishes to acknowledge
Jacqueline Palmer, Cecilia Walters,
Patricia Jackson, Zoë Hughes, Elaine Partington
and all others who have worked so hard to
bring this book to publication.

EDDISON · SADD EDITIONS

*Project Editor* Zoë Hughes
*Editor* Cecilia Walters
*Indexer* Dorothy Frame

*Art Director* Elaine Partington
*Art Editor* Jacqueline Palmer
*Design Assistant* Brazzle Atkins
*Line Illustrators* Simon Brewster and Anthony Duke
*Anatomical Illustrator* Gordon Munro

*Production* Charles James

The photograph on page 8 is reproduced by kind permission of Werner Forman Archive.

The photograph on page 129 is reproduced courtesy of Zefa Pictures Ltd.